BKM

WASHOE COUNTY LIBRARY

3 1235 01715 4928

P9-CJI-758

DATE DUE

GAYLORD			PRINTED IN U.S.A.

L.L. Bean

Canoeing Handbook

ALLAN A. SWENSON

The Lyons Press

Copyright © 2000 by L.L. Bean and Allan A. Swenson

All rights reserved. No part of this book may be reproduced in any manner without the express written consent of the publisher, except in the case of brief excerpts in critical reviews and articles. All inquiries should be addressed to: The Lyons Press, 123 West 18 Street, New York, New York 10011.

Illustrations © 2000 by Mitchell Heinz

For photography credits, see page vi

First Edition

Designed by Compset, Inc.

Printed in Singapore

10 9 8 7 6 5 4 3 2 1

Library of Congress Cataloging-in-Publication Data

Swenson, Allan A.
     L.L. Bean canoeing handbook / Allan A. Swenson.
        p.   cm.
     Includes index.
     ISBN 1-55821-977-3
     1. Canoes and canoeing Handbooks, manuals, etc. I. L.L. Bean,
  Inc. II. Title. III. Title: Canoeing handbook. IV. Title: L.L. Bean
  canoeing handbook.
  GV783.S94   1999

  797.1'22—dc21   99-41186
                                                                        CIP

Dedication

To my wife Sheila, whom I met when I was only 12 years old, in my first homemade kayak on Lake Swannanoa in New Jersey. She has patiently helped me paddle my way through life; in calm water, ripples, and rips, and some of life's whitewater challenges too, staying the course for 40-plus married years on canoe trips and ashore. It has been a richly rewarding adventure together.

Frontispiece: © Scott Spiker/Adventure Photo & Film
pg. viii   Courtesy Old Town Canoe Company
pg. 3   Courtesy Old Town Canoeing Company
pg. 4   © Scott Spiker/Adventure Photo & Film
pg. 6   Courtesy Wilderness Inquiry
pg. 7   Courtesy Old Town Canoe Company
pg. 8   © Bob Krist/Tony Stone Images
pg. 10   Courtesy Native Trails, Inc.
pg. 12   © Dennis Welsh/Adventure Photo & Film
pg. 13   © Paul Chesley/Tony Stone Images
pg. 14   © Scott Spiker/Adventure Photo & Film
pg. 22   (top and bottom) Courtesy Old Town Canoe Company
pg. 27   (top) Courtesy Old Town Canoe Company
pg. 28   Courtesy Old Town Canoe Company
pg. 30   © Jock Montomery/Adventure Photo & Film
pg. 31   Courtesy Old Town Canoe Company
pg. 32   Courtesy Old Town Canoe Company
pg. 33   (top) Courtesy Old Town Canoe Company
pg. 33   (bottom) © Layne Kennedy/Adventure Photo & Film
pg. 34   Courtesy Old Town Canoe Company
pg. 46   © Outside Images
pg. 49   © Mike Brinson Photography
pg. 50   Courtesy Bob Myron
pg. 51   Courtesy L.L. Bean
pg. 52   © Jock Montgomery/Adventure Photo & Film
pg. 58   © Charlie Borland/Adventure Photo & Film
pg. 60   © Mike Brinson Photography
pg. 61   © Jim Rowinski
pg. 63   © Mike Brinson Photography
pg. 64   © Jim Rowinski
pg. 67   © Jim Rowinski
pg. 68   © Gregg Adams/Tony Stone Images
pg. 70   © Wiley & Wales/Adventure Photo & Film
pg. 71   © Jim Rowinski
pg. 73   © Gary Brettnacher/Adventure Photo & Film
pg. 76   © Rick Ridgeway/Adventure Photo & Film
pg. 77   © Michael Javorka/Tony Stone Images
pg. 78   © Paul Harris/Tony Stone Images
pg. 80   Courtesy Hal Barter/Maine Department of Inland Fisheries & Wildlife
pg. 81   (top) Courtesy Tom Carbone/Maine Department of Inland Fisheries & Wildlife
pg. 81   (bottom) Courtesy Bill Cross/Maine Department of Inland Fisheries & Wildlife
pg. 82   Courtesy Bill Cross/Maine Department of Inland Fisheries & Wildlife
pg. 83,84,85   Illustrations courstesy Allan A. Swenson
pg. 87   Courtesy Old Town Canoe Company
pg. 88   © Art Wolfe/Tony Stone Images
pg. 90   © Mark Newman/Adventure Photo & Film
pg. 91   Courtesy Dennis Welch
pg. 92   © Mike Timo/Tony Stone Images
pg. 94   © Howard Grey/Tony Stone Images
pg. 99   © Jim Rowinski
pg. 102   © Jock Montgomery/Adventure Photo & Film
pg. 105   Courtesy Jackie Peppe
pg. 111   Courtesy Greg Lais/Wilderness Inquiry
pg. 112   Courtesy Old Town Canoe Company
pg. 118   Courtesy Old Town Canoe Company
pg. 124   Courtesy Old Town Canoe Company
pg. 126   Courtesy Old Town Canoe Company
pg. 128   Courtesy Allan A. Swenson
pg. 130   Courtesy Old Town Canoe Company

Contents

Photo Credits vi

Introduction 1

Chapter 1: Great Canoeing Adventures 5

Chapter 2: Canoe Essentials: Canoes, Paddles, and PFDs 15

Chapter 3: Canoeing Techniques: Solo and Tandem Paddle Strokes 31

Chapter 4: Canoe Clothing and Personal Gear 47

Chapter 5: Canoe Camping and Overnight Outings 59

Chapter 6: Enjoy Natural Discoveries, Wherever You Canoe 77

Chapter 7: Environmental Stewardship: Leave No Trace 89

Chapter 8: Canoeing Safe, Sane, and Secure 95

Chapter 9: Canoe Classes and Excursions for Beginners to Advanced 103

Sources and Information 113

Glossary 119

River Type Classifications 125

Acknowledgments 127

About the Author 129

Index 131

Canoeing is an American tradition.

Introduction

CANOES—AN AMERICAN TRADITION

The word "canoe" is a general term for a boat that has pointed ends and is open in the middle. It is designed for propulsion by one or more paddles, not oars, with the paddler or paddlers facing the bow. Curiously, the historical native name for certain types of boats used in the West Indies is "canaoa," a term similar to the French word *canot,* which translates as "boat."

Some of the earliest canoes were "dugouts," boats carved out of the trunk of a dead tree or one destroyed by fire. They were often beautifully carved and ornately decorated. Some were of considerable size and capacity. One giant dugout canoe, which now resides in the American Museum of Natural History in New York City, is 63 feet long, 8 feet 3 inches wide and 5 feet deep and was cut from a single log. So-called "war canoes" were dugouts used in paddling races in the South Pacific. Along the coast of West Africa, dugout canoes were used for fishing at sea for days at a time. Many of these giant canoes were also equipped with sails for longer trips.

Later canoes were constructed by Native American Indians of light, strong cedar frames over which animal skins or birch bark were stretched. The Inuit Eskimos followed a similar model, often using whalebone for the frame and seal or whale skin stretched over the outside. Today, most canoes are patterned after those that North American Indians made centuries ago. Indeed, the Penobscot tribe of Maine is credited with making the first canvas canoes in the 19th century, the precursors of the first Old Town canvas canoes.

Today's canoes may be made of wood covered with canvas, aluminum, or of resin, fiberglass, or even newer manmade materials. A modern twist on the old canoe is the *foldboat* canoe, a small collapsible boat of rubberized sailcloth stretched over a knockdown frame. These foldboats are easily transported for canoeing adventures on lakes and rivers far from home.

The most popular size canoes are from 16 to 18 feet long and anywhere from 30 to 34 inches wide. Wood canoes weigh about 60 pounds, depending on length. Aluminum and fiberglass canoes are usually lighter. Though a canoe will float in only a few inches of water, it can be carried, or *portaged,* from one body of water to another if necessary. Portaging allows canoers to bypass rapids or dams or to move from lake to lake in areas where connecting rivers don't permit canoeing.

The first books about canoeing were written between 1849 and 1869 by a Scottish lawyer, John MacGregor. His tales about his experiences on European canoe expeditions sparked widespread interest in canoeing in England, America, and in Europe. MacGregor was credited with being the inspiration for the launch of the Royal Canoe Club on the Thames River in July of 1865. He was the Royal's first captain. Among the Royal's early members were the Prince of Wales (who became King Edward VII) and Waringon Baden-Powell, founder of the original Boy Scout organization.

According to old records, the New York Canoe Club on Staten Island was founded in the later part of the 1800s, and by 1880, other clubs had formed all along the eastern seaboard. Cruising and competition between clubs prompted the organization of a national group to set standards and exchange information. The American Canoe Association (ACA) was formed at Crosbyside Park, Lake George, New York. W.L. Alden of the New York Canoeing Club was elected commodore and Nathaniel H. Bishop the secretary and treasurer.

Summer headquarters of the ACA was at Grindstone Island in the popular Thousand Island region on the St. Lawrence River. Its presence at that locale led to the formation of the Canadian Canoe Association, and some years later, the British Canoe Union.

To keep members informed, the ACA published *The American Canoeist* from 1882 to 1887. Arthur Brentano and canoeing enthusiasts Charles Norton, C. Bowyer Vaux, William Whitlock, and C.K. Munroe were among the journal's editors.

As canoeing gained in popularity, and competition between clubs increased, geographic divisions began to form. The Atlantic Division included the metropolitan New York area. The Central Division covered upper and western New York state and the Eastern Division included New England. New groups launched their own clubs or affiliated with the existing organizations.

After World War I, canoeing gained in popularity in continental Europe. In 1924, the Internationale Representationschaft des Kanusport (IRK) was successfully launched in Copenhagen. Also in 1924, a four-man canoe team from Washington, D.C., demonstrated a canoeing competition at the Olympiad in Paris. By 1936, canoeing was formally admitted to the program of the

Canoeing was one of America's favorite outdoor pleasures years ago and continues to grow in popularity today.

Olympiad held in Berlin. The United States and eight other countries sent teams for the nine different events held in 1936. Competitors were one- and two-man crews in various categories of rigid racing kayaks and canoes over distances ranging from 1,000 meters up to 10,000 meters.

When World War II began, the IRK dissolved amid the turmoil. However, when the war ended in 1945, the old organization reestablished itself as the International Canoe Federation (IFC), with 17 member nations. Canoeing competition became a fixture at the 1948 Olympic Games.

The Boy Scouts of America, the American Red Cross (as part of its Water Safety classes), the American Canoe Association, and other such groups began conducting canoeing classes for paddlers at all skill levels.

Perhaps the most colorful and exciting canoe events in this country are the professional and semiprofessional marathon racing events that have taken place over the years. To some, the most gruelling of these was the historic 450-mile Minneapolis Aquatennial Canoe Derby. The race followed a fast-paced route from Bemidji, Minnesota, down the Mississippi River to Minneapolis. The course covered the part of the Mississippi made famous by early explorers including Father Louis Hennepin, General Lewis Cass, Jean Nicollet, and Captain Willard Glazier. The Aquatennial is no longer run; however, many other such challenging races exist today. You can obtain details about entry to these events from local and regional canoe clubs and organizations such as the American Canoe Association or state tourist boards.

The canoe has had an important and ever-changing role in the landscape of American history. It has been a mode of transportation, a vehicle for athletic endurance and prowess, and a means to fun and adventure in the great outdoors. To learn more about the history of a canoeing and abroad, visit the References section at the end of this book or your local library or bookstore. To get started on your own American canoeing experience, read on!

There's a world of adventure awaiting you on America's waterways. Here, a family of four paddles on Lake McDonald in Glacier National Park, Montana.

CHAPTER 1

Great Canoeing Adventures

There are millions of miles of rivers and lakes to canoe all across America. Some are near your hometown; others offer exceptional wilderness adventures in exciting new locations. You may already have or know of favorite places to paddle in your state, but at some point you may want to explore waters farther from home.

Most canoeists like to expand their canoeing horizons, so I asked the expert instructors at the L.L. Bean Outdoor Discovery School (who helped provide much of the information for this book) to share their favorite canoeing places. You can find even more suggestions on the Internet. In my opinion the best Web site is that of the American Canoeing Association at **www.aca-paddler.org** (email **acadirect@aol.com**). From there, you'll be able to link with other informative sites, not to mention outfitters and clubs.

WILDERNESS INQUIRY ADVENTURES

One of the best canoeing organizations is Wilderness Inquiry, a nonprofit organization providing outdoor adventures for people of all ages, backgrounds, and abilities, including trips suitable for adventurous people with physical handicaps (see Chapter 9).

Wilderness Inquiry conducts trips all around the country, from Florida's Everglades to Maine's Allagash Waterway, from Ontario's White Otter Wilderness to the Boundary Wilderness Waters in Minnesota, and from Voyageurs National Park to Yellowstone National Park.

The Everglades canoe adventure takes canoeists through the only ecosystem of its kind in the world. One can paddle through miles of mangrove is-

Wilderness Inquiry conducts trips all over the country, from Florida to Maine to Yellowstone National Park and all points in between.

lands and lagoons in the shallow and protected *Ten Thousand Islands.* More than 300 species of birds abound; wildlife-rich estuaries and inlets allow exceptional opportunities for natural history exploration.

The *Ocklawaha River* in Florida offers canoeists trips down the crystal-clear waters of *Silver Springs* and *Juniper Springs* to the slow-moving dark water of the Ocklawaha River and the open water of *Lake George.* An array of animal and plant life awaits you in the surrounding *Ocala National Forest,* where the Tarzan movies of the 1930s were filmed. Legend has it that some of the monkeys cast in the movies escaped during filming and formed a colony. Today, their descendents swing from the branches of cypress trees near Silver Springs. Cormorants, egrets, and herons also populate the area. Cypress, holly, oak, magnolia, wild orange, and bay trees abound. Ospreys and eagles often pluck fish from the water as you glide quietly past.

For northern adventures, Wilderness Inquiry features three canoe excursions in Maine waters. The *Moose River,* flowing past Attean Mountain near the Quebec border, is noted for its beautiful scenery and relative isolation. Moose and other wild creatures add to the dramatic natural beauty surrounding the river.

Along the border of Maine and New Brunswick lies a series of wilderness lakes that form the headwaters of Maine's *St. Croix River*. These lakes offer a great introduction to wilderness canoeing as they wind their way through a maze of interconnected bays and islands. Paddlers can explore protected coves and inlets with rocky shorelines and hills covered with spruce forests in a pristine landscape.

Maine's *Allagash Waterway* is a 92-mile ribbon of lakes, streams, and rivers surrounded by mountains and lush forests. Renowned for its beauty and adventure, the Allagash offers opportunities to see many types of wildlife in one of the most dramatic, unspoiled wilderness areas of the East Coast.

Moving westward, the *St. Croix* and *Namekagon Rivers*, in northwestern Wisconsin, are part of the national *Wild and Scenic Riverway System*. Sweeping cut banks, tall pines, and deep pools characterize this remarkable area, with a bit of whitewater thrown in for excitement.

Another popular trip is Montana's *Missouri River*. Born in wild and open country the Missouri flows from the "Gates of the Rockies" onto the high Plains. The river flows past spectacular white sandstone cliffs that rise hundreds of feet above the water.

Canoeists enjoying the cascading display of a waterfall as they paddle in their Old Town Tripper canoe.

Canoeing past an escarpment on Buffalo River in Arizona.

The Missouri also crosses patches of the historic Nez Perce Trail, the route used by Chief Joseph and his people in their heroic attempt to outrun the U.S. Cavalry. Much of the route also follows the trail of Lewis and Clark on their historic journey nearly 200 years ago. Bighorn sheep on bluffs south of the Missouri Breaks are a natural history treat.

Even further west, the *Yellowstone National Park* canoe trip explores legendary Yellowstone on the largest alpine lake in North America. This land of soaring peaks, tranquil lakes, geysers, and grizzlies has captured the imagination of generations of adventurers. Travel to Yellowstone Lake in the heart of the park to experience true backcountry paddling. Trout fishing is exceptional, and the park's classic sites such as Old Faithful, Mammoth Hot Springs, and the Grand Canyon of the Yellowstone are awe-inspiring.

Red-rock paddling is featured in *Canyonlands' Green River*. There you can explore the striking beauty of the Green River in the desert country of the Southwest. This park is renowned for its stunning vistas and towering red-rock cliffs. From *Mineral Bottoms* the river flows through *Labyrinth Canyon,* where the inscriptions of early fur trappers and Native American petroglyphs are scratched side by side into the soft canyon walls. Paddlers pass the 4,000-foot Dellenbaugh Butte and the Hay Joe Canyon, and can marvel at the many majestic rock formations and ancient Anasazi Indian ruins that line the river's banks.

Wilderness Inquiry provides many more trips, including more tranquil, less taxing canoe trips for beginners and families. A three-day introductory canoe trip on the St. Croix River in 24-foot Voyageur canoes offers views of eagles and hawks soaring above sandstone cliffs.

NORTHERN FOREST CANOE TRAIL

The *Northern Forest Canoe Trail* stretches from upstate New York to the northern tip of Maine by way of Vermont and New Hampshire. This remarkable 700-mile waterway trail passes through historic towns and follows waterways and old portage trails used by Native Americans and European fur traders.

The Northern Forest Canoe Trail was researched, documented, and created as part of the vision of the founders of Native Trails, a nonprofit organization interested in preservation of our historic waterways. The three principal organizers, Mike Krepner, Ron Canter, and Randy Mardres, have collectively logged over 10,000 miles of paddling in North America to rediscover, chart, and travel obscure water routes.

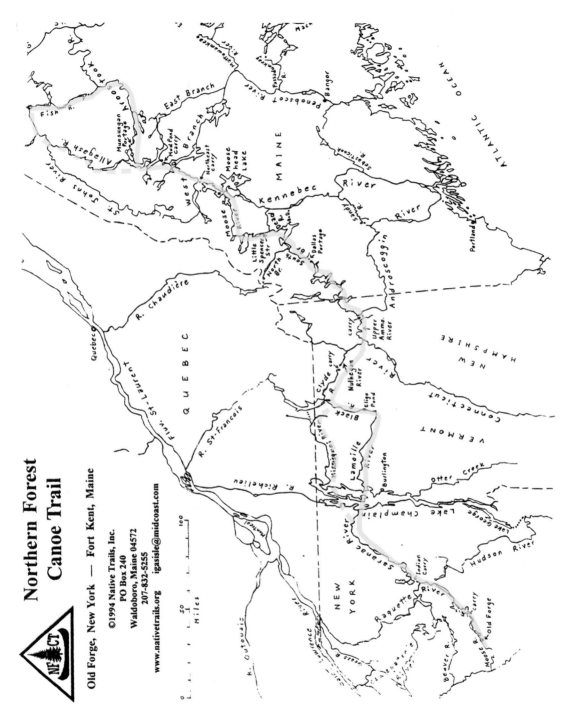

Northern Forest Canoe Trail

Old Forge, New York — Fort Kent, Maine

©1994 Native Trails, Inc.
PO Box 240
Waldoboro, Maine 04572
207-832-5255
www.nativetrails.org   igasisle@midcoast.com

The famous Northwest Forest Canoe Trail stretches from upstate New York to the northern tip of Maine.

Best Bets from The Outdoor Discovery School

The L.L. Bean Outdoor Discovery School canoeing instructors are chosen for their knowledge, skills, and ability to teach and lead exciting outdoor waterway adventures. They are all enthusiastic canoeists and seldom miss a chance to put their canoe in the water and paddle happily away.

These nationally recognized canoeing authorities kindly agreed to share their favorite canoeing places, not only in Maine (which is appropriately named "Vacationland, USA,") but also on various waterways throughout the United States.

Jackie Peppe, one of the most enthusiastic canoeists I've ever met, has concentrated her paddling all around Maine. One of her favorite rivers is the *St. Croix*, from Vanceboro to the flowage above Princeton, which is mostly flat with some easy rips with an easy portage around *Little Falls*. For a trip of a few days or several weeks, her pick is the *Allagash*. You can take your own canoe or have outfitters provide them at put-ins. They'll also pick you up at a designated time and place.

The *West Branch of the Penobscot* is another favorite. Peppe recommends reading Thoreau's *Maine Woods* before you go. A good variation on this trip for families with small children is to put in at *Lobster Stream* and camp on *Lobster Lake* for a few days. There's a nice sandy beach, which Peppe says is great for kids..

In the South, *Pearl River, Honey Island Swamp* in Slidell, Louisiana, has some fine day-trip possibilities, Peppe says. Late March or early April is the best for paddling through a climax forest, among the giant knees and trunks of cypress trees along the waterway.

For lake paddling, Peppe says the *Upper Range Pond* in Poland, Maine, has an easy put-in and is a fine spot during the week. Avoid it on weekends, she says, when jet skiers abound. You can pass under Range Road and paddle *Middle Range Pond,* do a portage across Rt. 26, and paddle all the way to the village of Poland.

Chesuncook Lake is Maine's third largest, with several nice campsites on it and many opportunities to explore nature from camp. From a campsite on Giro Island you can check out *Umbazooksus Stream* and *Lake* or *Black Pond* and *Caucomgomoc streams*. Or paddle up the West Branch of the *Penobscot,* or *Pine Stream*.

Bob Myron's favorite trips include the *Aroostook River,* from Oxbow to Washburn, and the *Madawaska Stream,* from Stockholm to Caribou, and the *Moose River.* For lakes, Myron recommends *Churchill Lake, Long Lake, Chesuncook Lake, Upper Richardson Lake,* and *Chamberlain Lake.* Always conscious of safety considerations, he reminds all that "(a) quick rain storm can drastically change the difficulty of any river and the wind is always a concern on the big lakes. Enter the wilderness with a careful eye on the elements for a safe and rewarding canoe trip."

Jamey Galloway's favorite trips include *Eagle Lake* and *Attean* and *Holeb* ponds because of the scenery and wildlife, her two key qualifications for places to canoe.

Ed Maillet, the L.L. Bean expert on canoes, paddles, and equipment, prefers Maine excursions. He likes the *Kennebec River* below the Forks, *Moosehead River,* the *Saco River* (in New Hampshire and Maine) with its marvelous sandy bottom, the *Sebago River,* and the *Flagstaff River.*

Karen Knight has led canoe discovery trips in far parts of the United States. Her favorite rivers are the *Green River* in Utah, and, for totally different ecology and environment, sections of the *Everglades Waterway* in Florida.

Kathy Kurz likes the *Saranac Lake* region of the Adirondacks, and suggests the *AMC Guide to Rivers* and *Delorme's Maine Gazetteer* as reliable resources to find great canoeing spots.

A couple paddling on a quiet pond in Vermont.

Details about the Northern Forest Canoe Trail and other rediscovered old-time canoe trails, including *Boundary Waters* in Minnesota, the *Coosa Trail* in Georgia, the *Eastern Ohio Trail* in Ohio, *Missouri Breaks, Potomac Heritage Trail,* and others are available from **Native Trails Inc., P.O. Box 240, Dept. MR, Waldoboro, Maine 04572**, or via the Internet at **www.nativetrails.org.**

As you plan your own canoe adventures, it pays to contact area canoe outfitters, as well as the American Canoe Association, Paddlesports, and other organizations. They offer a wealth of information, as well as guided and escorted trips.

Every state also welcomes tourists to come canoe, so consult the listings of state and Canadian tourism offices at the back of this book and be sure to give them a call before you set off. Or, just dip your paddle into the World Wide Web on the Internet to locate hundreds of great spots to launch your canoe. There's a world of waterways awaiting you.

Breathtaking scenery in Banff National Park, Canada.

The proper canoe outfit, one best suited to your particular needs, will ensure smooth paddling for years to come.

CHAPTER
2

Canoe Essentials: Canoes, Paddles, and PFDs

Whether you're planning a day trip or an overnight or longer cruise, a successful outing depends on matching the right equipment with the type of canoeing you intend to do. The most expensive outfit is worthless if it's not suited to your needs. There is no all-purpose canoe; however, most will adapt to a variety of situations. Others are designed for specific purposes such as competitive racing, whitewater canoeing, or carrying heavy loads for longer outings. When buying a canoe, always consider your primary purpose. Will you be using your canoe for cruising, day tripping, wilderness excursions, or just casual paddling on a nearby lake or stream?

CANOES

Canoes can be divided into the following general categories: *recreational, river running and tripping, touring,* and *sporting:*

- **Recreational Canoes:** Recreational canoes are suitable for a wide variety of activities. They are perfect for people who want to paddle their local lake, pond, or a quiet river. Some do have the performance features of more specialized canoes, but their stability and versatility make them an ideal choice for families and newcomers to the sport.

- **River-running and Tripping Canoes:** These are high-volume canoes designed for whitewater use and carrying larger loads on extended paddling vacations. They are *rockered,* with the ends higher than the center, for maneuverability and dryness, and they are built to withstand heavy abuse.

- **Touring Canoes:** Touring canoes tend to be more technical than general recreational canoes. They are normally long and narrow, designed for speed and efficiency. Although *initial stability*, the amount of stability when one first sits in the canoe, is somewhat reduced in a touring canoe, *secondary stability*, the amount of stability when leaning in the canoe, is enhanced. This type of canoe is versatile in a variety of water conditions, from calm lakes to moderate white water.

- **Sporting Canoes:** Designed for outdoor activities such as fishing and duck hunting, sporting canoes are stable, platform canoes with high initial stability. Some have square sterns for mounting a small motor. Others are designed to be paddled, rowed, or motored.

Canoe Materials

Canoe materials vary today, so you will want to consider durability, upkeep, weight, and cost. Always remember, more canoes are damaged by rough handling and improper storage than in actual use on the waterways.

Wood-canvas Canoes: Quiet and responsive wood-canvas canoes are a delight to handle. Before World War II, they were the only canoes available. Compared to all other materials, wood-canvas is fragile. Minor damage is easy to mend with inexpensive repair kits, but more serious damage results in difficult and expensive repairs, due to the hand labor involved. Maintenance and proper storage, which means elevating the canoe and covering it with a tarp, are required to prevent moisture penetration, which can cause rot and increase weight as the canoe absorbs water.

Wood Strip: Wood-strip canoes are built in small numbers. The usual construction is a series of wood strips, bent and glued together and covered with wood veneer (if not with fiberglass). Some models may also be covered with fiberglass. They require periodic relamination and upkeep to prevent rot. Damage repair is somewhat easier than with wood-canvas canoes. These "strippers" are probably the loveliest of all canoes and deserve pampering. Their delicate construction limits their use to flatwater paddling, however, and because they're handmade, these canoes also tend to be the most expensive.

Fiberglass: The general classification of "fiberglass" covers a wide range of canoe materials. Low-cost fiberglass canoes tend to be heavier. Medium- to high-cost fiberglass and *Kevlar* canoes tend to have more advanced and specific designs. Kevlar is similar to fiberglass, but it is a tougher fabric with more strength. Kevlar's light weight make these canoes excellent for longer wilderness trips. Fiberglass is the easiest canoe material to repair and is fairly maintenance free, although the outside gel coat will scratch and chip if you hit it hard against rocks.

A new material, *CrossLink3*, was developed by L.L. Bean. It is made using a patented, rotational molding process that offers exceptional value and superior strength. An interior layer of closed-cell foam is sandwiched between layers of cross-linked and high-density *polyethylene*, which gives the canoe extra strength, plus high inherent buoyancy. Even when filled with water it will float. That's a nice bonus!

This revolutionary new material and construction method is great for wear as well. Dents pop out easily and the material has a natural tendency to return to the original shape in which it was molded. It also has high environmental stress-crack resistance.

Aluminum: These canoes were the first no-maintenance canoes. Heavy-gauge aluminum canoes are fairly rugged. Drawbacks are the noise they make when scraped on rocks or hit with a paddle and their tendency to fetch up on rocks rather than slide over or around them. Aluminum canoes are impervious to the elements, which makes them a good choice if left out in the open. However, because newer materials offer many advantages in terms of handling and weight, aluminum canoes are less desirable and less readily available today.

Polyethylene-ABS: This material is the most forgiving. Polyethylene canoes tend to slide over rocks and bounce off them with little more than a surface scratch. Badly dented hulls, even those that have been bent around rocks, can be restored to their original shape, making these boats well suited for whitewater canoeing and rough handling.

The Anatomy of a Canoe

A canoe is the result of many interrelated design elements. Each element addresses a particular performance requirement; maneuverability, speed, paddling efficiency, stability, and cargo capacity. The performance of a particular canoe is determined by which design elements are emphasized.

Canoes are displacement craft. As they push water aside from the bow, they allow its replacement near the stern. The shape of the hull determines how efficiently the water is moved, and those that move water more efficiently are easier to paddle.

A canoe's overall performance is most affected by two basic measurements: length and width. The length of the canoe determines its potential speed. If two hulls are of equal width, the longer canoe will be faster and easier to propel. The shorter hull will be slower but easier to turn. A wider hull, especially at the *waterline* measurement, will generally be more stable than a narrower hull.

Length and width, combined with depth, determine the weight a canoe can carry and the size of the waves it can deflect successfully. That's especially important when sudden winds and storms whip up whitecaps and waves on a lake.

Beam: The widest part of a canoe.

Bow: The front section of a canoe.

Depth: The distance from the gunwale to the canoe bottom, measured at the canoe's deepest point.

Flare: The progressive widening of the hull from waterline to the gunwales that serves to deflect water and increase stability.

Freeboard: The distance between waterline and the gunwales; i.e. how much of the canoe sits above the water.

Gunwales: The rails along top edges of the hull that run the length of the boat.

Hull: The main body of the canoe.

Keel: A strip running the length of the canoe's bottom for the purpose of stiffening the hull and improving tracking.

Keel line: The shape of the hull bottom from bow to stern; it can vary from relatively straight to an extreme curved or "rocker" configuration.

Portage: Carrying a canoe between bodies of water or around obstacles during a trip; also, that portion of a trip where a canoe is carried on land.

Rocker: The degree to which a hull curves up at the end. A high rocker improves turning ability but decreases straight-line tracking ability.

Stability: Initial stability refers to the canoe's stability when a person first enters the canoe. Secondary stability refers to the canoe's stability when a person leans while paddling.

Stern: The rear section of a canoe.

Thwart: The crossbrace between the gunwales that helps keep the canoe rigid.

Tumblehome: The inward curve of the hull, from the widest point to the gunwales.

Tracking: The ability of the canoe to move in a straight line.

Waterline: The highest point that water reaches on the hull when the canoe is in the water, loaded or not. Important to check for safety on longer, more heavily loaded trips.

Yoke: A thwart shaped to allow the canoe to be carried on your shoulders during a portage.

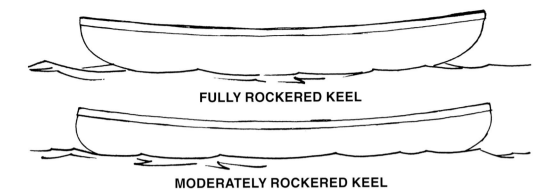

FULLY ROCKERED KEEL

MODERATELY ROCKERED KEEL

A basic understanding of the following canoeing terms will help you compare canoes and choose the right one for your needs.

Hull-shape differences can also greatly affect a canoe's handling characteristics. *Keel-line shape*, degree of *hull symmetry, cross-sectional shape,* and *above-waterline design* are among the most important performance variables.

Keel or Keel-line Shape: This refers to the shape of the hull bottom running from bow to stern. A straight keel line with minimal curvature will emphasize forward speed because more of the canoe's length is actually in the water. When the ends of the canoe's keel are curved or rockered, the canoe will maneuver more easily, because more of the canoe is out of the water.

Cross-sectional Shape: This refers to the outline of the hull viewed as if cut in half at its widest point. V-hulls offer the ideal characteristics for recre-

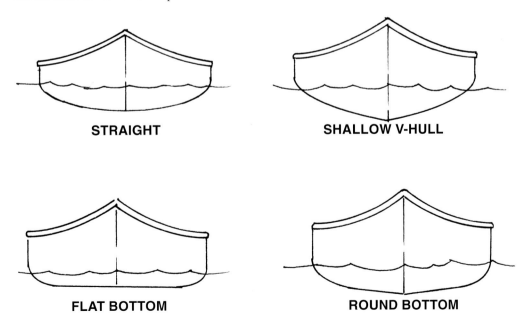

STRAIGHT   **SHALLOW V-HULL**

FLAT BOTTOM   **ROUND BOTTOM**

ational and all-around canoeing. Unlike a flat-bottomed canoe, which is stable only in still water, a shallow V-hull offers stability in moving and rough water, too. Beginning paddlers can learn to easily track a straight line and more experienced paddlers can lean the canoe to increase speed while turning.

Hull Design: Hull design, not necessarily the presence of a straight, external keel, determines how well a canoe will track in a straight line. For example, a shallow V-hull shape, when combined with varying degrees of rocker, provides both excellent tracking and maneuverability. A canoe with a flatter hull does not track as well.

Hull Symmetry: When a canoe has identically shaped horizontal halves with the widest point at the center, that design makes for predictable handling. In contrast, an asymmetrical canoe usually has its widest point a foot or more behind the center. In a straight-keel canoe, this shaple enhances forward speed, especially in shallow water.

Above-waterline Design: This refers to the two directions in which the sides of the canoe above the waterline can bend—inward, called *tumblehome*, or outward, called *flare*. Tumblehome allows the paddle to be more parallel to the keel for a more efficient *vertical stroke*, which helps the canoe track straight in flatwater cruising. With flare, the sides extend outward above the waterline, to deflect water and give greater stability in heavier waves.

With these terms in mind, you can select the canoe that will suit most of your canoeing adventures. Before you shop, make an honest evaluation of your intended needs and uses. What types of canoeing activities will you be

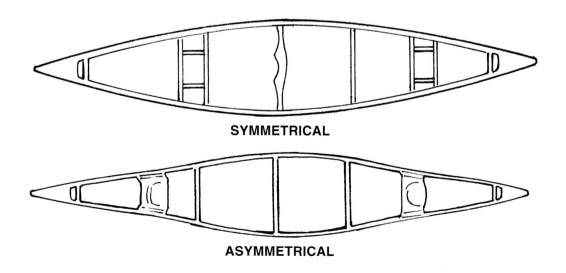

SYMMETRICAL

ASYMMETRICAL

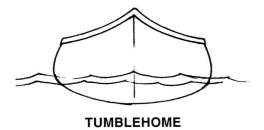

TUMBLEHOME

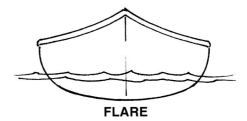

FLARE

doing most of the time? Will you paddle mostly on calm lakes and ponds or in waves and white water? Do you prefer a stable fishing canoe? Do you plan to explore wilderness rivers yourself, or with others? Do you want to move up to canoe racing and competition? Will you be taking longer trips with your entire family? When shopping for a canoe, keep these general principles in mind:

- **Length:** The average canoe is about 16 feet long. Longer canoes generally have greater hull speed, increased carrying capacity, and track better. Shorter canoes, although not well suited for long trips or heavy loads, are lighter and more maneuverable.

- **Width:** The width, or beam, is given in two measurements: at the gunwale and at the 4-inch waterline. A canoe carrying an average load sits about 4 inches deep in the water. That measurement has the greatest influence on performance. Wide-beamed canoes offer greater stability but are usually slower. Narrow canoes may be less stable but offer greater efficiency and speed.

- **Hull Shape:** Flat-bottom canoes offer great initial stability and feel very secure on calm water.

  - *V-Shaped hulls* have less initial stability but good secondary stability. As the canoe is leaned, it will balance on its side and resist further tipping. V-hull or shallow hull designs work well in waves where the wind can lift the canoe up suddenly. A V-hull will help tracking in short canoes and improve the canoe's resistance to crosswinds. V-hulls or molded keels also work well on canoes used with small outboard or electric motors because they decrease sideslipping. However, a keel would not be preferred on a canoe used in white water or situations where quick maneuvers are required.

  - *Round-bottom* canoes have great secondary stability but little initial stability. They are designed for speed and efficiency.

Best Bet Canoes

Here is a list of some recommended canoe models, compiled with the help of Ed Maillet and the staff at the L.L. Bean Outdoor Discovery School:

- For all-around use by novices, the 16-foot *Penobscot* model made by Old Town Canoe Company is perhaps the best multi-use canoe on the market. Made with Oltonar-Royalex, a lightweight yet durable ABS laminate, and crafted with a straight keel line, the Penobscot is a versatile family canoe. The Penobscot's design and construction make it very much at home in fast water as well as flatwater. The 16-footer is fine for tandem day tripping and also handles well as a solo canoe for paddlers with higher-level skills who enjoy some downriver whitewater or wilderness trips. At less than 60 pounds, it is easily loaded and portaged, its load capacity is rated at 860 pounds.

This canoe is available with an optional center seat that adds an extra passenger spot for family outings. Its straight-on speed, easy handling, and load capacity are the qualities an all-around performance canoe should offer.

The 17-foot *Penobscot* by Old Town Canoes offers more speed and ease of handling with a larger load capacity, up to 1,100 pounds. Yet at only 65 pounds, it can still be transported easily out of the water. The Penobscot's sharp V-hull bow and fast, shallow-arch bottom give this canoe its unique capability.

The Penobscot 16-foot canoe is one of the most popular and versatile canoes for individuals and families.

- If you're looking for a lightweight, stable design, the *Osprey* by Old Town appeals to sportsmen, older couples, and families who need a durable, lightweight canoe. Constructed of Oltonar-Royalex, this canoe tracks well and is available in portage or rowing versions.

- For those who want smaller, more easily portable canoes, the *Stillwater* 12- and 14-foot canoes by Old Town feature wide and deep bodies that are easy to manage, even by youngsters.

Some canoeists favor the light weight and durability of the Old Town Osprey canoe.

- Another good choice is the *Katahdin* 12-foot, with a 750-pound load capacity. The keeled design of this canoe tracks well even in challenging crosswinds, yet its light weight makes it easy to transport.

The *Explorer* line of Mad River canoes also are highly recommended and popular and have a surprisingly useful load volume.

- The *Explorer* model, made of Royalex, is highly rated as an all-round canoe. From day outings to wilderness trips, for tandem performance or solo use on placid lakes or white water, the 16-foot Explorer has become a favorite of beginners and experts alike. With a shallow V-hull design, it tracks well and has good secondary stability in rough water conditions.

- The fiberglass version of the 16-foot Explorer combines more affordable material with the excellent paddling performance of the Explorer design. It is stable and secure, and can carry ample gear for a casual afternoon paddle or extended outing. The fiberglass 16-footer has sharper bow and stern profiles than its Royalex counterpart; some believe this design makes it a better gliding canoe for lakes and gentle rivers.

- Another 16-foot Explorer is made with Kevlar, the tough fiber used in bulletproof vests. This lightweight canoe has tremendous structural strength in comparison to its fiberglass counterpart. It has very high durability and minimal weight—only 51 pounds—with an aluminum gunwale system for structural support.

- If weight is a high priority, an even lighter 16-foot Explorer (the Lightweight) is available. This boat has a stiffer and efficient paddling hull with aluminum gunwales. At only 39 pounds, the Lightweight is ideal for seniors or those who cartop or portage frequently.

- Mad River also makes a wide variety and range of other canoes, including the 14-foot *Winoosk,* a wide-bodied, very stable canoe, and the *Tahoe 14,* which offers exceptional initial stability and sense of security for sportsmen and casual canoeists.

Lincoln Canoes are noted for their light weight. Their Paddle Lite Kevlar process, utilizes a vacuum-bag, resin-infusion laminating process so the entire boat is laminated under vacuum for the ultimate strength-to-weight ratio. One of their best is the *Hidden Pond* canoe, named because it is a "very big, small canoe" designed to be easily carried back to a "Hidden Pond." The 12-foot model carries up to 850 pounds yet weighs only 37 pounds. The 14-foot model carries up to 1000 pounds but weighs only 45 pounds.

Bear Creek Canoes, another excellent canoe maker, offers sturdy, lightweight canoes in various models and sizes, including a 10'6" *Little ME* model, a good choice as the first canoe for younger members of a family. The 14-foot *Wide One* has a 42-inch beam that offers greater stability for fishing and hunting trips.

For those with high-level canoeing skills, Old Town, Mad River, Lincoln, Bear Creek, and other firms offer their own special versions of canoes designed specifically for racing, whitewater, and long-range excursions.

When you shop for your canoe, use the information in this book to ask questions. As you've probably gathered by now, there are many different styles, materials, price ranges, load capacities, and special design capabilities. Today, your choice of canoes is wider than ever and modern construction materials make canoes even more durable and low maintenance than ever before.

PADDLES

The canoe paddle has a long history dating back to early Native American Indians and their birch bark canoes. Early trappers spent many hours carving their own paddles to fit their individual needs. As years passed, the famed Maine Guides became the primary users of canoes as they traveled into wilderness areas with their clients. They soon discovered that a variation in paddle length, blade shape, grip design, and material could contribute to the comfort and efficiency of paddling for long journeys on flat water, or maneuvering on dangerous rapids found along their waterways in the remote north woods.

Although paddle design has evolved, some early paddle designs continue to be produced today because they are efficient and functional. Modifications of traditional designs have produced special paddles for advanced canoeing. Whatever type of canoeing adventures you prefer, it is best to pick the right paddle and invest in the best you can afford. A paddle is your propulsion system and your source of power. Other than your boat, nothing is more important. As you shop for paddles, consider whether you are hard on equipment. Do you paddle a lot in shallow rivers? Is your hand size bigger or smaller than average? Match the right paddle to the condition of the water you expect to paddle and to your own ability and strength.

Paddles today are divided into two categories, *straight shaft* and *bent shaft*. Within these categories you have your choice of material, including traditional wood, laminated wood, fiberglass, or Kevlar cloth incorporated into the blade construction. You also have your choice of paddle shape. I strongly

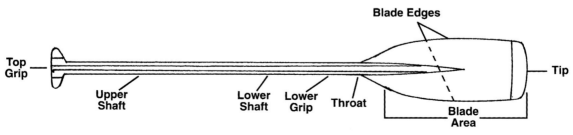

The anatomy of a canoe paddle.

recommend buying an extra paddle. Your "spare" can be the same type, or a different type if you wish, so you can have different types for different paddling situations. Naturally, always take your spare paddle on every trip.

Sizing the Shaft

Shaft length is the most important measurement in selecting a paddle. The traditional measurements for paddle length call for a paddle that reaches from your toes to your chin for the bow paddler, and from your toes to your eyes for the stern paddler. Another way to determine a proper paddle fit is to sit in a canoe with the paddle blade almost throat deep in the water. The paddle's top grip should then be at your shoulder level. The paddle blade should be fully buried in the water at mid-stroke. A paddle that is too short wastes energy; one that is too long will be awkward.

However, while paddling solo, you may need to execute a powerful brace or draw stroke, which requires a paddle several inches longer than one used for tandem paddling. A long paddle with a narrower blade, for example, is best suited for executing numerous "J" and "pitch" strokes (see next chapter). Shorter shafts are good for quick strokes on flat water and reduce the wide-arc recovery time in white water. (The sooner the blade can return to the water, the sooner you can begin your next stroke, which may be vital in boiling rapids.)

Bent-shaft paddles are increasingly popular. Modern bent-shaft paddles were first developed by racers who wanted the straightest, fastest ride. The effectiveness of a bent-shaft paddle can be explained by focusing on what happens to a canoe when it is driven forward by a conventional paddle. Initially, blade power is directed downward. Then, as the paddle completes its arc through the water, the force is directed upward, causing the canoe to bob fore and aft, which reduces speed. With the bent shaft, the blade's arc is modified so that a greater proportion of forward thrust is maintained during the latter part of the stroke. This reduces bobbing. The bent shaft blade attains peak efficiency with short, quick strokes. For sizing, a bent-shaft paddle should be 2 inches shorter than your straight-shaft paddle size.

Outdoor Discovery School canoe instructor Kathy Kurz prefers a bent-shaft wooden paddle for flatwater paddling. For freestyle flatwater play she favors a straight-shaft Grey Owl wooden paddle. For white water and scratchy shallow streams, Kurz likes a durable synthetic straight-shaft paddle. Instructor and guide Bob Myron prefers a laminated wooden bent-shaft paddle with a pear grip for flatwater touring and a Mitchell wooden paddle with a T-grip for white water.

Paddle Materials

Today canoe paddles are made in one-piece wooden models, wood laminates, and combinations of aluminum shafts and synthetic blades and handles. You have a wide range of choices available. Price depends on quality, durability, and construction. Traditional one-piece wooden paddles are constructed of ash, maple, or spruce. Wood provides a warmth and spring, or *flex*, to the paddle. Many canoeists like that feel and believe it makes paddling easier.

Spruce is the lightest and least expensive wood but it tends to be stiffer, more brittle, and less strong. Maple is the sturdiest, quite flexible but heavier. Ash is a good compromise between the relative stiffness of spruce and the weight of maple. Maple and ash paddles should never be left in sun because their blades can warp in excess heat.

Wood-laminated paddles are light and easy to wield. They are often available in increments of 1 or 2 inches, so choosing just the right length is not a problem. There is less *whip* or flex in laminated paddles, but they are rugged, long lasting, and less likely to break than standard wood paddles. They are also more expensive. Woods used in laminates may include spruce, hickory, mahogany, ash, cherry, and cedar, in varying combinations.

Synthetic paddles are made of aluminum or high-tech synthetics such as fiberglass or Kevlar. Their best features are strength and durability. Although they lack the whip of wood paddles, their light weight is an advantage, making them less tiring to use over a long distance or several hours of paddling time.

Picking the Best Blade

Paddle blades are available in different shapes and widths. A narrow blade, 5 to 6 inches across at its widest point, is easier to draw through the water than one 8 inches or wider, but narrower blades give you less *purchase*, or grip, on the water. That means more strokes are needed per mile and you get a slower response from the canoe. A wide blade drives a canoe faster and brings about a quicker response. However, it is more tiring to use because of its increased resistance in the water. If you like racing, an 8-inch blade works well, but if you're planning to paddle for hours at a stretch, a 6- to 8-inch blade is preferable.

Blades are available in four basic shapes:

- The **oval** blade is very popular. Generally this blade has a relatively short overall length—about 48 to 62 square inches—for quick, powerful strokes.
- **Square** or **rectangular** blades are common among laminated wood and fiberglass paddles. The bottom of the blade is cut off square and often a horizontal piece is then fitted across it for reinforcement and protection.

ls ___
le ___
ll ___

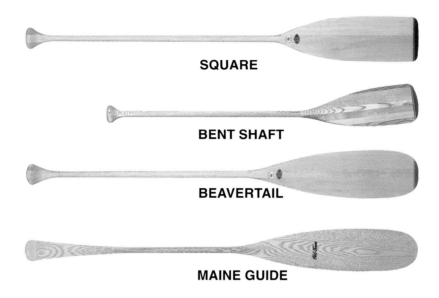

SQUARE

BENT SHAFT

BEAVERTAIL

MAINE GUIDE

The square corners provide greater bite in the water, but they are noisier and not suitable for quiet paddling.

• The **beavertail** paddle, named, of course, because it's shaped like a beaver's tail, and the **Maine Guide** paddle, which carries its width farther up the blade, both provide good purchase and are quiet as well as graceful. These usually are somewhat more expensive than conventional wooden paddles.

Canoeing instructor Jamey Galloway likes the wooden Grey Owl (an oval blade) for flat water and Wooden Dagger for white water. She adds that the larger the blade, the more power you get. But a larger blade may be tiring on a long trip. Larger blades are good for white water and freestyle play canoeing, but a smaller-bladed or more traditional beavertail shape is good for touring.

Paddle Grips

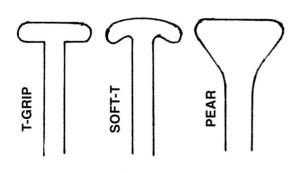

T-GRIP   **SOFT-T**   **PEAR**

There are several different types of grips available. Grip selection is a personal choice. You may prefer the classic **oval, pear shape,** wider **Maine Guide,** or a more modern **T-grip.** The best way to pick a grip is to test them all and get the one that is most comfortable for you.

For smaller women and younger family members, small grip and shaft paddles may be best. T-grip paddles are useful when you want more control or leverage, especially in fast water.

PERSONAL FLOTATION DEVICES—PFDS

Personal flotation devices (PFDs), commonly referred to as life jackets, are designed for one purpose only: to save your life. You'll find many styles and weight-carrying capacities, so an understanding of the options is essential to picking the best for you and each member of your family.

PFDs are designed as a life-protecting device to be used by canoeists and anyone else who enjoys various types of boating activities. They are worn to assist in floating or swimming when a watercraft is overturned. Different boating conditions determine the type of PFD you should be using: check the appropriate U.S. Coast Guard and individual state regulations. State regulations may be more stringent than U.S. Coast Guard standards, so you should check them for the state where you plan to canoe.

In many states PFDs are mandatory, even in canoes. Generally, laws require that PFDs be carried aboard all watercraft. Accidents can happen quickly: a life jacket in the bottom of a canoe or tucked away with gear will do you no good if you capsize. Trying to put on a PFD in the water is difficult and almost impossible in rough water or if you are injured. Don't take risks. Always wear your PFD from the time you step into the canoe until you are ashore again.

The Coast Guard has five type classes of PFDs. Only two (Type II and Type III) actually apply for canoe use. PFDs are classified by their minimum buoyancy ratings; using standard weights of 22, 15½, 11, and 7 pounds to determine a

There is a personal flotation device (PFD) made for everyone in the family, big and small.

PFD's class. Because the human body is lighter in water, the standard weights have been calculated to match individual weights when suspended in the water.

1. Type 1 PFD has the greatest required buoyancy. It is designed to turn most unconscious persons in the water from a face-down position to a vertical or slightly backward position. These PFDs are designed for adults weighing more than 90 pounds and children weighing less than 90 pounds. Type I PFDs are recommended primarily as the best PFDs for offshore and ocean waters. This type is not usually recommended for flatwater or even whitewater canoeing, but if you do other types of boating, Type I PFDs can do double duty.

2. A Type II PFD is any approved wearable device that is designed to turn its wearer in a vertical or slightly backward position in the water.

3. A third category, Type III PFD is any approved wearable device designed so the wearer can turn himself upright in a vertical or slightly backward position. While these PFDs have the same buoyancy as the Type II, they have little or no turning ability. They are available in a variety of styles, colors, and sizes. Some styles also provide increased hypothermia protection.

New designs of PFDs, available at canoeing and sporting goods stores, meet U.S. Coast Guard standards and are more comfortable and less restricting. Some even provide warmth during cooler weather canoe trips. Properly fitted PFDs should not impede motion and should keep your head well above the water and protect you from bruises, floating objects, or natural structures. Your PFD should fit snugly enough with a drawstring or belt to secure it properly in place so that it cannot slip free over your head.

I prefer my bright yellow Stearns, Comfort Flex, SolarMax PFD. It fits snugly, allows free arm movement and adjusts for comfort. A bright color, yellow or orange, may clash with natural wilderness surroundings, but will make it easy for rescuers to spot you in an emergency. Try on different types and simulate various canoeing strokes to be sure your own PFD will be comfortable as you paddle. Some PFDs recommended by veteran canoeists include Lotus, Cacheted, and Extrasport brands in various sizes for proper fit and comfort.

PFDs should be dried and cleaned after each trip to preserve their life-saving capacity. If you have any doubts about your PFD's serviceability, discard it and replace with a new one.

Wearing a PFD is the most important measure you can take towards safe and sane paddling. You should be wearing one any time you are on any waterway. There's no excuse not to.

Learning and perfecting proper technique makes canoeing safe and a lot more fun.

CHAPTER 3

Canoeing Techniques: Solo and Tandem Paddle Strokes

Before you set off on any canoe trip, solo or tandem, you must first get your canoe and yourself on the water. Be careful while unloading the canoe from your vehicle, especially from a roof rack. Once the canoe is on the ground, always lift with your legs so you don't strain your back. Always put on your personal flotation device (PFD) before you launch your canoe. Most overturns or capsizes occur getting into or out of a canoe at the shore or dock.

It takes two people to unload a canoe safely and easily from the roof rack of a car.

Proper single-person carry.

Boarding Your Canoe

There are some basic techniques to remember when boarding your canoe:

1. Keep your center of gravity low.
2. When putting in or launching from a steep bank or dock, place your boat in the water alongside and parallel to the shoreline or dock. Hold on to the dock as you enter the canoe.
3. Squat down next to your canoe. Carefully shift your weight over the centerline while holding onto the gunwales. Step the foot closest to the canoe onto the centerline and quickly kneel down. You can add stability by holding your paddle perpendicular across the top of the boat as you enter it.
4. Tandem paddlers should board one at a time and stabilize the boat for one another. You can launch from ankle-deep water in the same fashion if you prefer.
5. When launching from a beach, you can also use the above boarding method. Some prefer to have the bow of the canoe pushed up on shore and the stern in the water. Carefully board and move to the stern seat and sit down. Your body weight lifts the canoe so the bow paddler can board as the stern paddler stabilizes the canoe with a paddle on the shallow bottom of the stream or lake.

When boarding a canoe, remember to keep your center of gravity low. Tandem paddlers should board one at a time and stabilize the craft for each other.

Preparing the canoe. Larch Lake, Minnesota.

MASTERING THE BASIC STROKES

You are the power behind the paddle. The more you master the right strokes, the easier your canoe trips will be, especially on longer excursions. Anyone can stick a paddle in the water and propel their canoe. But when you become proficient in a variety of different strokes and practice to perfect your technique, you'll have better control of your canoe and save energy, too.

Because canoeing is such a fast-growing family sport, we will assume for the duration of this lesson that there are two paddlers in the canoe, paddling on opposite sides. As you are learning new strokes, both you and your boat-mate should try to stick to paddling on your designated sides until you have perfected the strokes. Only then should you switch the paddle to the opposite side. This will help you learn the strokes faster.

The first step is to make sure you're holding the paddle correctly. Choose the side of the canoe on which you wish to paddle. That becomes your *on-side*. Your hand holding the top of the paddle, or grip, is your *grip hand, or control hand*. That hand controls the angle of the blade. Your other hand is the *shaft hand*. Space your hands comfortably, about shoulder-width apart, with your arms mostly straight.

When practicing, *don't change your control hand grip*. All strokes should be executed simply by rotating your control hand and wrist to set the appropriate paddle positions for each type of stroke. Always keep the same side of the paddle facing you. That side is called the *power face*. Usually the paddle will have a brand name on one of the faces. It's helpful to use this as identification of the power face. If there is no brand name on the paddle, paint or tape one side of your paddle blade to identify the power face.

When learning new strokes, you and your boat-mate should each stick to your chosen side of the craft. Agree to switch sides after you've each perfected the strokes.

All strokes include three phases: *catch, propulsion,* and *recovery.* All strokes, with the exception of the *pry* and *reverse one-quarter sweep,* use the power face of the blade for propulsion. Most paddle blades, except bent-shaft paddles, do not differ from one side to the other, but our intent is to get you to always use the same side of the blade for power.

There are several basic principles for achieving maximum efficiency from a paddle stroke. For maximum power, the blade should be perpendicular to the force of water resistance. In other words, when you want to move the canoe forward, hold the paddle vertically, so that the power face of the blade faces flat toward the stern of the canoe.

As you apply power through your stroke, be sure that the blade remains perpendicular to the water surface. Any changes of angle of the blade will lead to a turning motion or create lift of the water. Consequently this will waste energy if you are just trying to canoe straight ahead.

A second important principle is to face your work and apply power from your major muscle groups. You'll soon discover that you have much more strength and endurance in your back and shoulders than in your arm muscles alone.

By rotating your torso and unwinding through each stroke, you will go further than you would from just pulling on the paddle with your arms. Another key fact: by rotating your torso in this way you will also avoid shoulder strain and injuries. When you're learning, watch the blade throughout each stroke. Once you gain experience, you'll be able to rotate your body effectively while you're looking off in any direction to enjoy the scenery or spot wildlife.

There are basic strokes you should learn in order to control your canoe properly and easily, whether paddling solo or in tandem; in the bow or stern. These strokes can be grouped into *turning strokes* (to turn your canoe), *power strokes* (for forward or reverse direction), and *abeam strokes* (to move to either side).

Solo and Tandem Paddling Strokes

Forward stroke: This is the basic power stroke for solo or tandem paddling. It moves the canoe forward in a straight line. Hold your paddle perpendicular to the water and close to the side of the canoe. Using your shoulders, back, and arm muscles, move the power face of the blade to the rear of the canoe in a short, straight line. Lift the paddle out of the water and return to the forward starting position. Keep your paddle close in to the side of the canoe and perpendicular to the water. The power face should be facing the stern during the entire stroke (see illustration on p. 36).

1

2

3

4

Forward stroke.

For a forward stroke, keep your arms straight during the *catch position*, the point when the blade enters the water, so you can get a "grip" on the water. The paddle shaft should be vertical and your upper body should be rotated so if the paddle is on the right, the upper body should be facing the left side of the canoe. For propulsion, unwind your torso and stop the stroke at your hip. A short, quick stroke of about 10 to 12 inches is best. At the end of propulsion, your upper body ends up facing the paddle side of the canoe. For recovery, rotate your paddle parallel to the canoe as it slices through the air to its original catch position for another forward stroke. You can also *feather* the blade (turn it parallel to the canoe) in the water to quietly return to the catch position.

J-stroke: This also is a variation on the forward power stroke used by the stern paddler or solo paddler to provide forward momentum. It helps the canoe maintain a straight line of travel.

J-stroke.

As you master the J-stroke, you'll soon discover the ease of keeping a straight course with very little effort. The J-stroke is a corrective measure used at the end of a forward stroke. To make a J-stroke, the catch position is the same as a forward stroke, and the propulsion is the same in relation to your hip position. Once the paddle is near your hip, rotate your control hand until your thumb points down to the water. Push the paddle blade away from the boat, keeping the blade in the water as you push water away from the boat with the power face of the paddle. After your stroke has brought the bow back in a straight line, feather the blade or lift it out of the water as you prefer, and return to a catch position.

If you are doing the J-stroke properly, you should feel your forearms stretching when you turn your control thumb down to the water. Use this stroke when you must overpower the bow person or the canoe is turning to the side the bow paddler is paddling on.

Common mistakes are turning your control thumb up rather than down, not keeping the blade vertical in the water, and not leaving the blade in the water when you push away from the canoe. That push away is the actual turning part of the J-stroke.

Forward sweep and reverse sweep from the bow.

Forward sweep and reverse sweep from the stern.

Forward sweep: This stroke is for forward motion and turning. A sweep describes the same arc as the canoe's gunwale. For a bow paddler, this stroke begins at the hip, and finishes at the side of the canoe. For the stern paddler, a bow sweep starts with the paddle extended toward the bow and finishes at the hip. Sweep strokes are somewhat more difficult. There are two types: forward and reverse sweeps, depending on which direction you wish to turn the canoe.

Forward one-quarter sweeps: These are probably easier on the arms and torso. For the bow paddler, start with the paddle blade in the water as near to the bow as possible, with the paddle shaft horizontal to the water. Sweep the paddle away from the canoe in a C motion and stop the stroke when it is perpendicular to your hip. For recovery, rotate your control thumb so it points toward the bow and feather the paddle back to catch position.

As the stern paddler, start the stroke at a right angle to your hip, holding the paddle shaft horizontal to the water. Sweep your stroke to the stern and recover with your control thumb pointing away from the canoe. For both bow and stern paddlers the power face should be facing the stern during the stroke.

Reverse one-quarter sweep: This stroke actually uses the backface of the blade, not the power face. It is merely the reverse of the forward one-quarter sweep. With a bow paddler using the reverse one-quarter sweep and stern using a forward one-quarter sweep, the canoe pivots to the paddling side. If the strokes are reversed, the canoe pivots to the non-paddling side.

Draw stroke: This is an abeam stroke used to pull your canoe sideways toward the paddle. Extend your upper hand out over the water; your control hand should be no higher than your forehead, keeping the paddle shaft vertical to maintain a safe paddle position. The lower (shaft) hand provides the propulsion by extending and pulling the paddle in toward the hull. This stroke can be done by the bow or stern paddler. If done simultaneously on opposite sides, the canoe will turn on its axis in a circular motion.

Slice the paddle back to its original position. Rotate your control hand so your thumb points toward the stern of the boat and repeat propulsion. All power in this stroke comes from the bottom or shaft hand pulling in. The top (control) hand stays extended out over the water. Actual propulsion need only be about 10 inches.

Draw to the bow: This is a bow stroke only. For the catch position, rotate your control hand so your control thumb points down to the water. Your shaft arm and paddle shaft are aligned as one; you should feel that you are looking at your wristwatch on your control hand. Once in this position, set the blade in at a 45-degree angle to the bow. The blade should be vertical in the water and the shaft more horizontal. For propulsion, unwind your upper body and pull the stroke toward the

Draw stroke.

Draw to the bow.

Draw to the stern.

Cross-bow draw stroke.

bow until the paddle hits the front of the canoe. For recovery, just lift the paddle out of the water and return to the catch position.

Draw to the stern: Rotate your control hand so your control thumb points up to the sky. Set the paddle blade behind you at a 45-degree angle to the stern with the blade in the water. For propulsion, pull the paddle toward you until the paddle blade touches the stern end of the canoe. For recovery, rotate your control thumb away from the canoe so the paddle will feather back through the air to your catch position.

Cross-bow draw stroke: This is the term for a regular draw stoke done on the *off side,* the side opposite the one that the bow paddler is usually paddling. To execute this stroke, begin in the catch position by lifting the paddle blade over the boat to the other side without changing the position of your hands. When bringing the paddle over your canoe, rotate your control thumb so it points up at the sky. Set your blade in the water at a 45-degree angle to the bow. The blade should be vertical in the water. For propulsion, pull the blade toward the bow of the canoe until it hits the tip of the canoe. For recovery, pick the blade up out of the water and return to the catch position. This stroke is an option for the pry stroke (see next page) in the bow. Remember that although you cross over the canoe and are paddling on

1

2

the same side as your partner in the stern, you have not changed your hand positions on the paddle. That way you can immediately go back to the other side and continue regular paddling. This stroke enables you to maneuver more quickly to your nonpaddling side.

Pry stroke: This stroke, which some canoeists call a *side stroke,* is used by the stern paddler for both sideward movement and for turning. It can be used in the bow, too; however, it is not as powerful as the draw stroke. In effect you push the blade away from the canoe, or *pry* the water as you would a piece of wood with a crowbar. The canoe will move in an opposite direction from the blade movement.

For the catch position, the power face of the blade should face you with the

3

Pry stroke.

shaft vertical and the blade positioned right next to your hip, just as it would be at the end of a draw stroke. Lock the thumb of your shaft hand on the gunwale. For propulsion, using the gunwale as a fulcrum or lever, pull your control hand down to your lap. This will push the blade away from the boat. For recovery, push your control hand forward toward the thwart, as if you were rowing, until you can slice the blade back into the water near your hip at the catch position.

PRACTICE CANOE MANEUVERS

Once you have perfected your basic canoeing strokes, put them together with a partner to develop better canoe maneuvers. Combine these strokes and you'll soon be a veteran canoeist.

For forward motion, use the forward stoke in the bow combined with the J-stroke in the stern.

To pivot to the paddle side, both bow and stern paddlers should use a draw to the hip. Or, the bow can do a draw to bow and the stern a draw to the stern. You also can accomplish a pivot with the bow doing a reverse one-quarter sweep and the stern paddler doing a forward one-quarter sweep.

For pivots to the nonpaddling side, bow and stern can both do pry strokes. Or, the bow can do a cross draw while the stern paddle does a pry. In addition, the bow paddler can do a forward one-quarter sweep while the stern does a reverse one-quarter sweep.

To "sideslip" a canoe to the side the bow person is paddling on, the bow would do a draw to the hip while the stern paddler does a pry.

If you wish to sideslip a canoe to the side the stern person is paddling on, the bow can do a pry while the stern does a draw to hip. You also can achieve this with the bow doing a cross draw while the stern does a draw to the hip. Another way is for the bow paddler to do a cross draw while the stern does a draw to the stern.

With a bit of practice, you'll gain the experience to make canoeing easier, less strenuous, and more fun.

Tips on Capsizing

As you experiment and practice, keep in mind that eventually you may flip or capsize your canoe. Most tipovers occur as people are boarding a canoe from shore or dock. If that happens, simply wade back to shore or use the dock to climb out of the water.

If you are in a canoe away from shore and it capsizes, simply fall out, assuming that you are properly wearing your PFD, of course. With a PFD, you won't need to worry about staying afloat.

Try your best to hold on to your boat *and* paddle. If you're in moving water, aim to float on your back with your face up and your feet on or near the surface of the water. Even in fairly shallow water, a river can be dangerous if your feet become wedged under a rock or hidden snag.

While you hold your canoe and paddle with one hand, use the other hand to do a side stroke toward the nearest shore, eddy, or landfall. Resist the instinct to stand up, especially in moving water or in water that is over knee deep. Wait until you are out of the current and the water is very shallow. Even then, it is best to crawl out on to the shore to avoid any underwater potholes or snags that may trip you.

You can also attempt to re-enter your canoe on the water. Follow these steps to re-enter a swamped boat:

- If the canoe is upside down, first reach over the bottom of the hull and grab the opposite gunwale. Pull it toward you to right the boat.

Re-entering a capsized canoe.

Rocking a boat dry.

- Put your paddle into the canoe and then boost yourself up over the gunwale at either end of the boat. When your hips are over the gunwale, simply twist your body so you can roll into the water-filled canoe.
- Stay seated on the bottom of the boat and paddle to shore. If the paddle has drifted away, use your hands to paddle to shore.

If the canoe is upright but too water-filled to paddle, follow this basic procedure to empty it:

- Swim to one end of the canoe and press down on that end. Push the canoe hard away from you so that movement flushes some water out. You may need to do this several times.
- Then, swim to the middle of the side of your canoe.
- Hold the side down and push it away, again flushing out water so only a small amount remains.
- Then, re-enter your canoe.

If you have fallen overboard for any reason and the canoe is still upright and dry, or you have rocked the boat almost dry, follow these tips to re-enter an upright canoe. Basically, it is the same maneuver, but a bit more difficult because the canoe is riding higher in the water. Grasp the gunwales with both hands; one on the furthest gunwale and one on the nearest. Then kick your legs to propel yourself forward as you pull with your hands and roll into the empty canoe.

If you and your canoeing partner have both gone overboard, have one person stay in the water to help stabilize the canoe while the other re-enters. The partner in the canoe should then lean in the opposite direction to balance the canoe as the partner in the water re-enters.

It pays to practice these maneuvers on a sunny day in warm water so you will have the skills handy in the event that you will need to re-enter a capsized canoe in open water.

Re-entering an upright canoe.

Naturally, if you are near shore, you can simply turn the capsized canoe over while standing in the shallow water and re-enter it. With a partner, empty the canoe, right it, and stabilize it as one person gets in and stabilizes the canoe with the paddle as the other re-enters.

If you are traveling in two canoes and one capsizes, follow these basic steps to right the capsized canoe:

- Position the capsized canoe upside down and perpendicular to the upright one.

- The person in the water should press down on one end of the hull of the capsized boat. This will elevate the opposite end of the canoe out of the water.

- Push the capsized canoe's bow or stern up over the gunwale of the upright canoe as the person in that rescue boat pulls the upside-down boat up over the gunwales until it is emptied of water.

- Then, slide the empty canoe back into the water, keeping it upright.

- The person in the rescue canoe should stabilize the righted canoe by kneeling in the middle of the upright canoe and holding the gunwale of the righted canoe until the person in the water can re-board it.

It makes sense to practice canoe rescues in warm weather to perfect your skills on this basic maneuver, too. It is best to learn these skills from a qualified canoeing instructor. Hands-on lessons will speed up your learning process dramatically. The Outdoor Discovery School at L.L. Bean and American Canoeing Association instructors nationwide offer many classes every year (see Chapter 9). Sign up and tune up your canoeing skills in every way. And don't forget to put on your PFD and bring an extra paddle every time before you push off.

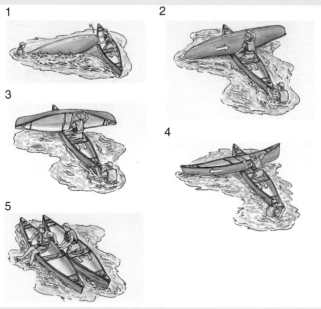

How to perform a canoe rescue.

Today, a canoeist's life is much improved by everything from high-tech materials used for canoes and paddles to the lightweight designs of sleeping bags, tents, and stoves. This group packs up gear before heading off for a few days on Lobster Lake, Maine.

CHAPTER
4

Canoe Clothing and Personal Gear

When voyageurs and other fur trappers began exploring America's western frontiers, they did it by water route. They were hardy souls and by today's standards their equipment was rudimentary. They usually traveled in a 26-foot Canot du Nord or 36-foot Canot du Maître, paddling with hand-made hardwood paddles they carved themselves. Each man carried a knife, a fishing line to catch food, a small iron pot for cooking, flint and steel to start fires, and a trusty rifle for hunting game and protection.

For sleeping they used wool blankets or fur skins from the animals they had trapped. Clothing amounted to woolen pants, a shirt or tunic, and wool socks, with an extra pair for bad weather. Most trappers had fur jackets or handmade garments of animals skins for cold weather wear.

When I first began my own canoe adventures in an ancient, yet still water-worthy wood-canvas Old Town canoe, my gear was an Army surplus tent, a canteen, a field cook kit and utensils, a down-filled and patched Army sleeping bag, a rain poncho, a flashlight, some matches in a sealed tin (pipe tobacco can), and a Red Cross First Aid Kit.

A canoeist's life is better today, with greatly improved canoes, paddles, PFDs, nutritious trail mixes, and portable stoves. We can choose from a variety of lightweight tents, down sleeping bags, and many other useful items to ensure a satisfying trip. I like it much better this way. So do the millions of people who take to the waterways every year. Sure beats fur trapping!

According to Paddlesport Industry estimates, Americans spend more than $60 million annually on canoeing, including equipment, gear, equipment rental, outfitter-guided trips, and other costs related to canoeing vacations. To help you have a pleasant, comfortable, safe and rewarding canoe experience, I've collected some of the best advice from veteran canoeists, members of the ACA, and the L.L. Bean Outdoor Discovery School instructors.

At the end of this chapter, you'll find convenient checklists of gear and clothing to bring on day trips and longer trips. Copy the lists and use them whenever you canoe.

THE KEY THREE—WWW

Because proper clothing is a basic factor in canoeing comfort it helps to understand the "WWW" system of layering, sometimes called "onioning." Dressing in layers of light clothing gives you the flexibility to stay outdoors longer through changing weather. You can easily control your comfort by adding or removing a layer. Building a layering system for yourself is easy if you understand the principle: Stay warm but don't overheat. Stay dry and protect yourself in heat-stealing environmental conditions. To achieve this state of warmth and dryness, follow the three W's of Layering: **weather**, **warming** and **wicking**.

Weather

The outer layer of your clothing is the one that meets the weather head on. It is your first barrier of protection against the cold, wind, and rain. The degree of protection is a direct result of this layer's wind and moisture resistance, its thickness, type of insulation, and its length.

Supplex nylon fabrics offer excellent wind protection and water resistance in mist, light rain, and even light snow. Gore-Tex provides water repellency while allowing moisture to escape. In most clothes of this fabric, all exposed seams are sealed against leakage. Some new types of coated fabrics are designed to be completely waterproof; however, many are not breathable and are not recommended for highly active, strenuous sports. Details about different fabrics are included at the end of this chapter.

Warming

Warmth comes from the middle layer of fabric sandwiched between your outerwear and the layer of fabric against your skin. Fleece and pile are the functional favorites because they are soft, warm for their weight, and dry more quickly than wool or cotton. Because they pull moisture to the surface, they work well in combination with the crucial inner *wicking* layer. Polyester fleece

Layering your clothing, using the "WWW" principle, is the key to staying dry and comfortable for hours at a time.

or microfleece in pullover jacket or vest are best bets. A wool or down jacket can be added for extra warmth.

Wicking

The inner or wicking layer will keep you warm and also dry. Keeping this layer dry is critical. Damp clothing against the skin can leave you permanently chilled, no matter what the weather. Underwear made of knit polyester is better than cotton because it doesn't retain moisture. Synthetic underlayers actively "wick" or pull moisture away from the skin. They also dry more quickly, reducing the risk of hypothermia. Silk underwear is also a popular choice.

The wicking layer is probably the most important factor in dressing for outdoor activities. Veteran outdoors adventurers have long recognized the need for protective underwear. Select the proper underwear to match your intended activity level—one set of insulating underwear will not be appropriate for all outdoor activities. Physically active paddling dictates the need for fast-drying fabrics that will transfer body moisture away from your skin. Less strenuous activity, such as quiet paddling, requires underwear of higher insulating value. A common mistake is to put on long underwear that is much too heavy for the day's particular activity. It is wise to go light with undergarments and layer up or down as situations dictate.

PROTECTING YOUR EXTREMITIES

As you consider adjusting your comfort level for outdoor adventures, remember weather can change quickly and drastically. Don't forget your head, hands, and feet. A head without a hat is much like a house with an open window. Your head, especially around your temples, is the easiest place for body heat to escape. A hat can be one of the best garments for controlling your body's temperature. If you are paddling strenuously, just take your hat off and let excess heat escape. When you stop, put your hat back on to trap heat.

Hands and feet also benefit from proper heat control. Adding a polyester wicking layer underneath gloves and socks keeps fingers and toes dry and protects them from discomfort and frostbite during early spring and late fall expeditions. Never wear cotton in the cold, because it tends to stay wet longer, robbing your body of valuable heat.

Canoeing shoes or comfortable, reliable sneakers with nonskid soles are my favorite footwear in most seasons. In cooler early spring and late fall

Pick a comfortable hat that keeps the sun (and rain!) off your face and neck, as Outdoor Discovery School canoe instructor Bob Myron does.

weather, lightweight hiking books are handy, especially for excursions inland around campsites and for other explorations along waterways. I always pack an extra set of camp moccasins or shoes for wear around the evening campsite, or if my basic shoes get wet for any reason.

Neoprene gloves and booties can be a lifesaver in cold, damp weather.

BASIC CLOTHING CHECKLIST

Whether you elect to obtain a whole new wardrobe for your canoeing expeditions or add a few items now and then as budget permits, is your choice. As you plan your future canoeing adventures, including longer trips, especially into wilderness waterways, here's a composite checklist, based on recommendations from veteran canoeists and Outdoor Discovery School instructors and guides:

- Wide-brim, waterproof hat—for warmth and sun protection
- Bandanna
- Stocking cap for colder days
- Gloves and/or mittens
- Waterproof boots or canoe shoes
- Camp shoes or moccasins—to protect fragile campsites from erosion
- Spare shoelaces
- Gore-Tex socks
- Synthetic or wool socks
- Pants (long and short, for changing conditions)
- T-shirts, polo or jersey shirts
- Long-sleeve shirts—for layering and to thwart bugs
- Sweatshirts or fleece shirts/jackets
- Underwear (synthetic wicking type best)
- Belt and/or suspenders
- Windbreaker or wind/water-resistant outer shell garment
- Rain pants and jacket

- Sunglasses
- Swim suits and towels
- Watch (waterproof)

GEAR AND ACCESSORIES

Proper clothing is one basic consideration for a successful canoeing adventure. Another is the right gear. The Boy Scouts have a well-proved motto, "Be Prepared." That's a key to remember.

Here's a two-part canoe trip checklist. Some items are recommended for every trip, such as PFDs, compass, maps, water container and water purification system, portable stove, tent, tarp or fly, and sleeping bags. Others are important for longer trips. These lists are the result of combining many checklists from different canoeing authorities, instructors, and others who have spent years guiding canoeing excursions, especially in remote wilderness areas.

As the Boy Scouts of America motto instructs, "Be prepared." Before you head out on the open water, make sure you've loaded your canoe with all the clothing and gear you'll need.

Checklist for Day Trips

- Canoe
- Paddles (including an extra paddle)
- PFDs—*one for each participant*
- Maps—area and topographic (keep second map separate)
- Highlighter or map-marking pen
- Waterproof map case
- Compass—*one for each participant*
- Dry bags for waterproof storage
- Plastic trash bags (so you Leave No Trace)
- Stuff sacks for storage
- Day pack or other backpack for hikes afield
- Yoke pads for portage comfort
- Whistle or horn for communications and emergency—*one for each person*
- Seat pads and cushions if desired as extra PFD aids
- Rescue throw bag and 50-foot line
- Sponge and bailer
- Bow and stern lines
- Elastic bungee cords for securing items
- Camp stove and fuel
- Pocket and camp knives
- Water containers and water purification system
- Basic cooking pots with lids and frying pan
- Eating utensils—metal or durable plastic
- Kitchen knife and cooking/serving utensils
- Plates, drinking cups
- Pot holders and scrubbers
- Dish towels, paper towels, and dishwashing supplies
- Biodegradable soap in waterproof container or bottle
- Matches in waterproof case, backup lighter source
- Camp saw and axe
- Aluminum foil and plastic zip-lock bags

- First Aid kit
- Animal, plant, bird identification Pocket Guides
- Animal track-casting kit
- Notebook, diary, nature sketch pad
- Pens and pencils (pencils can easily be sharpened by your pocket knife)
- Camera (waterproof, if possible) and film, in waterproof camera bag
- Pocket tripod
- Binoculars
- Reading glasses and spare set of regular eyeglasses
- Sunglasses for all, with a cheap spare pair
- Lip balm and sunscreen lotion
- Bug repellent (whatever you have found best for your body chemistry)
- Toilet paper
- Personal hygiene supplies
- Prescription medications and Aspirin/Tylenol/what you prefer
- Wallet with money and credit cards
- Driver's license and another personal photo ID
- Jumper cables for vehicle, just in case
- Copy of your Float Plan (*Leave a copy with a friend or relative and a ranger or warden*)
- Packable multipurpose fishing kit
- Fishing hand drop lines, hooks
- Weather radio and extra batteries
- Pocket Survival Tool
- Multiblade Swiss Army knife—*one for each individual*
- Nalgene water bottles—*one for each person*
- Whatever else makes you happy and at home in the wilderness!

Checklist for Overnight and Longer Trips

- All **Day Trip** items plus:
- Wheeled canoe carrier
- Tents as you prefer (larger for time inside during buggy season)
- Rainfly, for eating comfort

- Tent and fly stakes, poles, ties
- Ground clothes and mattresses
- Sleeping bags—your personal choices
- Folding camp chairs or dual-purpose cushions
- Lantern with spare mantles and fuel
- Several flashlights, extra bulbs and batteries
- Water bag or bucket for larger groups, longer trips
- Bowls, mixing cup, and spoons
- Toilet articles, razor, pocket mirrors
- Extra rope, to bear- and critter-proof food
- Petrol head lamp
- Playing cards, books
- Mini stove and lantern combo kit
- Portable sink
- Snorkel gear

WHAT DO THE PROS WEAR?

The Outdoor Discovery School staff who have guided many trips under all types of weather and water conditions offer some additional thoughts about their favorite clothing and accessories.

Jackie Peppe suggests nylon shorts and a Coolmax T-neck or tank top. In cool or wet weather she adds a short-sleeved, coated nylon pullover. In cold weather, she adds long johns and a long-sleeved, coated nylon paddling top. If it is really cold, she may add a layer of fleece under the paddling top and wear coated nylon paddling pants. She emphasizes that she always wears a PFD, which adds plenty of warmth, too.

Her footwear on quiet water and/or warm weather trips tends to be bare feet. If it's cold or she's paddling moving water, Peppe likes neoprene booties with a flexible sole for kneeling.

Kathy Kurz lists lightweight and quick-drying clothes for warm weather and water, such as the L.L. Bean tropic-weight shirt, sport shorts, a hat with a visor, and sunglasses. She usually brings along a synthetic long-underwear top as a wicking layer, a wool or polar fleece sweater as a warming and insulating layer, and a breathable Gore-Tex rain and wind shell, plus a wool or polar fleece hat to wear if the weather gets chilly.

In cooler weather, Kurz adds some wool or polar fleece pile pants, with a lightweight pair of synthetic long underwear bottoms or cool weather running tights under a pair of rain and wind pants. Some neoprene paddling gloves or neoprene or nylon poggies are also useful.

In cooler weather and water, especially moving and white water, she suggests a wetsuit under a paddling jacket or rain and wind jacket, or a drysuit with the appropriate wicking and warming layers underneath. She also emphasizes the importance of a hat and paddling gloves or poggies as well as a PFD at all times.

For footwear in warm weather, Kurz opts for Teva or other water sandals or aqua sox that can be slipped off in the canoe, old sneakers or water shoes. In cooler weather, she wears a pair of wool or neoprene socks under the old sneakers or water shoes. Neoprene booties with tough soles are a good choice, she says. She is especially fond of high rubber boots, such as the L.L. Bean Wellingtons or fishing boots or the high-top L.L. Bean boots, worn with synthetic liner socks and heavier wool socks, because "it's nice to step in and out of a canoe floating in cold water and keep your feet dry."

Bob Myron favors the Penobscot Paddler shoe, worn with neoprene socks when it's cold, without socks when it's warm. To keep his feet dry, he prefers Bean boots. Myron's choice of pants are the L.L. Bean ripstop climber pants or ripstop nylon quick-drying pants. Blue jeans are his least favorite pants for paddling, because they are heavy when wet and cotton dries slowly. The Bean tropic-wear shirt is his favorite because it drys fast, keeps sun and bugs off, and is cool enough to wear all summer.

Jamey Galloway prefers a nylon long-sleeved fly fishing shirt with SPF or polypro shirt or a short-sleeved Coolmax shirt in summer. For cool conditions she adds a wool or fleece jacket and a wide-brimmed hat. Jamey also recommends nylon quick-dry pants (the rock-climber type with the snap at the ankle) or nylon shorts in summer, sometimes wool or fleece pants in colder conditions. She urges canoeists to look for clothing that is non-constricting, comfortable, and quick drying; ideally, it also affords some protection from the sun.

Her footwear favorites for touring in spring or fall are 16-inch Bean boots and, in summer flatwater, Merrill or Teva water sandals. She is still looking for the perfect all-around paddling shoe. Her qualifications are something comfortable to wear while sitting and kneeling. Neoprene will help keep your feet warm if they get wet.

Important Information on New Clothing Fabrics

Many new fabrics have become available during the past decade. Knowledge about these fabrics lets you ask focused, educated questions when shopping!

- **Activent:** A water-resistant and breathable fabric similar to Gore-Tex.

- **Aquastretch:** A special form of Thermal Stretch made by Wyoming Wear. It is composed of a layer of fleece laminated to a layer of polyurethane to make it warm, fuzzy, stretchy and both water- and windproof.

- **Bipolar:** A material woven by Malden Mills. It works by increasing the surface area on the outside of the fabric without increasing inside surface area, so the cloth moves moisture away from your skin.

- **Coated Lycra:** A urethane coating that makes material waterproof while retaining its usual stretchy ability.

- **Dryflo:** A bi-component fabric from Lowe Alpine Systems. The inside and outside surfaces are of different surface areas, so water is wicked from the inside to the outside.

- **Gore-Tex:** A layer or membrane that is laminated to a textile to make a waterproof but breathable fabric. The membrane has pores that are larger than water vapor molecules but smaller than liquid water molecules. Thus, vapor can pass through but liquid water cannot.

- **Neoprene**: Flexible rubber filled with tiny bubbles that make it soft, stretchy, and buoyant and a good insulator.

- **Oxford:** A plain-weave fabric often used for paddling clothing because it has good water-shedding ability.

- **Ripstop:** Refers to a lightweight fabric that has a grid of heavier yarns woven into it to help stop tears from spreading.

- **Taffeta:** A lightweight weave in which heavier flat yarns are woven in one direction to produce a fabric with very high tear strength.

Setting up camp on the shore of a scenic lake is a perfect way to close a day of exploration and exercise on the water.

CHAPTER
5

Canoe Camping and Overnight Outings

Camping is one of the added delights of canoeing. Cooking a meal by the side of a lake and listening to loons call while the aroma of fresh fish rises from your frying pan is one of life's prized pleasures. The sounds of the forest, a whippoorwill call, a fox bark, the croak of a bullfrog, and the thrill of seeing wild critters and creatures in their native habitat continue to inspire all those who paddle America's waterways and camp on their shores.

Before you venture afield, plan ahead. Use a topo map, guide book, and local knowledge to plan your lunch and rest stops and to locate your overnight campsite *before* you get underway. You can find sources for dozens of river and lake canoeing spots and campgrounds in this book and you can look up details on the Internet at various Web sites provided by the American Canoeing Association, Professional Paddlesports Association, L.L. Bean, and various U.S. Government agencies. (See Chapter 9 and the Sources and Information section.)

Consider the terrain, water supply, sanitation needs, and a cooking plan. Check to see if your campsite needs to be reserved in advance or is available on a first-come, first-served basis. Always have a backup plan if your primary site is taken when you get there. Be certain to obtain the necessary fire permits, if open fires are allowed, and also any other permits you may need in the area you'll paddle and camp.

Other key considerations include bug conditions, weather, prevailing winds on lakes, the distance you must travel to reach your campsite, and sleeping comfort. Weather can change rapidly in the wilderness, so be aware and plan for both the best and worst.

When setting up camp, find a well-drained, flat site. Clear it of stones and debris. Place a ground sheet under your tent, to save wear and tear on the tent floor and to keep it clean. You may also wish to put a plastic sheet on the inside of your tent to make the floor super watertight.

Look around you when you pitch camp. Look up for "widow makers," as old time woodsmen call them, dead branches stuck in live branches that might dislodge in wind storms. It usually pays to find a site out of strong winds, but a lighter breeze is generally welcome, to keep bugs away.

Look around for a well-drained, flat site before you pitch your tent. Note bug conditions, strong prevailing winds off waterways, and any "widow makers."

TENTS, TARPS, AND SLEEPING BAGS

Because you can carry more equipment on a canoe trip than a backpacking trip, you can enjoy a roomier tent, a cooking fly, and roomier sleeping bags and other campsite equipment. Most camping supply stores or the experts at L.L. Bean can provide you with advice to help you select what is best for your needs.

Selecting Tents and Sleeping Bags

If you are shopping for a tent, you have a wide range of sizes and styles available. For canoeing camp trips, the lighter and more roomy the better, especially if you hit a period of bad weather and must spend more time inside your tent than you had planned. Obviously cost is a factor, but when selecting a tent, it is usually best to buy one that is easy to set up, lightweight, and guaranteed waterproof. You should also select a tent with screening tight

Don't "skimp" when buying a tent. It's your home in the wilderness and your best defense against the elements. If you buy the best tent you can afford, it will pay you back with years of reliable service.

enough so that the smallest gnats and no-see-ums can't squeeze through. Don't skimp on your "home" in the wilderness. Insist on solid construction, sturdy supports and tent poles and stakes to secure it well, especially in wind and rain storms.

Like a canoe, a tent is a lifetime investment, so get the best you can afford. Modern dome tents snap into place quickly and can be staked down to withstand winds. Those with add-on rooms are handy.

Choice of sleeping bags is both a matter of personal comfort and dependent on the type of weather you'll have when camping. Some people prefer mummy bags; others like roomier rectangular bags. Sleeping bags are rated for temperature. Pick the best bag rated for the temperature range of your most common types of campouts. Consider more insulation if you like to bundle up when sleeping. Ground cloths, covers, and mattresses add comfort but also need cleaning, periodic inspections, and maintenance.

Make sure that you have proper insulation under your sleeping bags with a Therm-a-Rest air mattress or closed-cell foam pad. Even small stones or roots can be very uncomfortable without a good ground pad. Consult the camping checklist at the end of this chapter to be sure you include the ground cloths and eating or rain flies, plus stakes, sturdy poles, shelter accessories, and the sleeping bags you prefer for the particular season as you plan each trip. Pack a

Outdoor Discovery School canoeing instructors have their favorite tents and sleeping bags, selected from their years of canoeing experience.

- Bob Myron prefers a Sierra Designs Meteorlight tent, a summer-weight (40°F) Mt. Washington sleeping bag, or a Feathered Friends down bag for fall, with a Hydroseal stuff sack. Myron likes an Ultra Light Therm-a-Rest, as in *Camping* guide sleeping pad.

- Jamey Galloway likes the L.L. Bean Ultralight 3 to use as a two-person tent and the Sierra Designs Meteorlight as a one-person or small two-person tent. For sleeping bags, she recommends a synthetic-filled bag such as the Mt. Washington bag. For spring and fall use, she has a Feathered Friends down bag and is careful to keep it dry in a triple bag. Galloway thinks down is fine for water trips, providing one is careful to keep it dry, because down has the best weight-to-warmth ratio of any fill. She uses a Therm-a-Rest LE, which is very light.

- Jackie Peppe and Kathy Kurz both like the three-person Light Stuff 3 tent and the Mt. Washington 20° mummy sleeping bags with Therma Rest Deluxe LE pads. Ed Maillet and Diane Day, who has taken numerous extended canoe trips, suggested the Woodland's four-person tent, a 12 × 12 foot ground cloth tarp, Mt. Washington 20° sleeping bags and Therma Rest pads.

Air out sleeping bags and tents before and after use. You'll be glad you did!

large enough tarp and lines to cover your kitchen area and to keep you dry if it rains.

Care and Maintenance

After every trip, and before your next one, check all your gear, including tents, tarps, and sleeping bags. Naturally, you should follow the manufacturers' instructions for care of your equipment, but here are some basics to remember.

Keep your tent clean. Wash any dirt off your tent with a sponge or in a tub with warm water and mild soap. Hang it to dry thoroughly before putting it away and store your tent in a dry place out of sunlight. Nylon material does not support mildew, but a urethane coating can. Once urethane mildews, the coatings peel off, rendering your tent no longer properly waterproof. Also seal seams if needed, stitch or patch tears, and fold shock-corded poles from the center to reduce stress on the cords.

Hang sleeping bags to dry after trips and air them out before new excursions. You can clean most with a mild soap and warm water in a commercial-size washer. Hang synthetics to dry or use an air cycle dryer. Dry down sleeping bags in a large dryer on air (fluff) or warm setting.

Although you'll seldom need big backpacks for canoeing trips, you should also check whatever ones you use before and after each trip. Clean packs as you would a tent. Keep pockets zipped at all times in the field, so no rodents or small critters can enter to explore them.

Set loaded packs down easily to avoid bursting seams or breaking a frame. Loosen all straps before putting a pack on or taking it off to save energy and frustration too.

There are many different choices for padding to fit underneath your sleeping bag. No matter which kind you choose, some form of padding is always recommended.

SETTING UP CAMP AND PREPARING MEALS

Be sure to set up camp in established campsites or set up so you disturb the land as little as possible. That includes using a "cat hole" for human waste, dug well away from the waterway and actual sleeping area.

Plan your meals thoughtfully. Remove all unnecessary cardboard and paper packaging from foodstuffs before you leave home. Place all dry ingredients such as sugar, spices, and powdered foods in zip-lock bags. It helps to pre-measure amounts for each meal for cooking convenience. Pre-combining ingredients for making meals is helpful too. Use masking tape to label contents of each zip-lock bag, unless the contents are obvious. Add cooking directions in the bag, unless you carry your own pocket cooking guide.

Pack crushable and breakable foods such as breads, crackers, candy bars, cheese, and fruit in rigid containers. A cardboard milk container works well and it can be burned when you're finished

Keep Foods Cool and Fresh

Before you leave on your trip, read these helpful tips I've collected from veteran canoeists and my own personal experience, with thanks to the Coleman Company for some additional tips:

- Pre-chill food and drinks. Each 12-oz. six pack or gallon of liquid will use about 1 ½ pounds of ice just to cool from room temperature. Cool everything before you head out. Remember that cold air travels down, so if you want your vegetables well chilled, load cans and bottles first, then cover with ice. Keep coolers out of the sun. Ice lasts up to twice as long when kept in the shade. Crushed ice or cubes cool food and drinks faster, but block or large chunk ice lasts longer.

- Don't drain cold water. Even melted ice water keeps food and drinks cold and preserve remaining ice much better than empty air space. It pays to consider two separate coolers; one for beverages you'll want frequently and another for the bulk of your food. Place perishable goods like meat and dairy products directly on ice. If sealed in plastic containers, they'll stay dry, even in ice water.

- Remember that you may want to save some hot drinks or food. Wide-mouth thermos bottles are handy, but don't use plastic jugs as containers for hot liquids. Leftover food stored in new-type microwave, sealable containers can be heated in a pot of hot water.

- Keeping food containers and beverage coolers clean is important. Before and after using, clean both the inside and outside with a solution of mild soap and warm water. To remove tough stains, use baking soda and water. You can remove odors with a diluted solution of chlorine bleach and water. If odors persist, wipe the interior with a cloth saturated with vanilla extract, then leave the cloth in the cooler overnight. Always air-dry containers with the lid open before storing.

with it. Other rigid containers include your coffee pot, Rubbermaid or Tupperware containers and gallon or five-gallon plastic buckets.

Pre-slice vegetables and seal them in zip-lock bags. If you prefer not to pre-slice to retain the freshest flavor, don't forget a cutting board and kitchen knife! Liquids are best carried in plastic bottles with screw caps. Nalgene bottles don't leak and are especially useful. Put creams, jellies, jams, and peanut butter in Tupperware or wide-mouth Nalgene jars.

Another idea is to pack all elements of each meal together and seal each in a gallon zip-lock bag or other container. Label each meal: "Monday dinner," etc. If you pre-pack meals with perishable items, put the meal in a cooler, add a layer of ice, then another meal in its plastic bag, and a layer of ice until the entire cooler is filled. Naturally, put the last meal you need on the bottom of the container and work backwards. That minimizes the time the cooler is open allowing ice to melt.

FOOD AND MENU IDEAS

Canoeing takes energy, whether you're paddling for stretches in calm, flat water or driving downstream with the current. Staying energized and well nourished is like maintaining a campfire. Any good fire starts with kindling. Once it starts, we add some mid-sized sticks and then logs for the long burn.

When canoeing, start out by snacking on simple carbohydrates such as sugars and fruit, which your body will burn quickly. Once you have enjoyed those, add some complex carbohydrates like breads, grains, and pastas. Then add the meats, cheeses, and veggies for further nourishment. Carbohydrates are the primary energy source and should be consumed every 30 to 45 minutes on the waterway.

One favorite and reliable food for waterway nutrition is a tasty bag of gorp, which stands for Good Old Raisins and Peanuts. I mix up a batch of my own at home and separate portions into zip-lock bags.

My recipe is equal parts raisins, M&M candies, dry roasted, unsalted peanuts, and multibran Chex. A handful or two of multigrain Cheerios goes well, too. Dried cranberries add extra taste. You can also buy prepared trail mixes at camping stores and health food shops, but I prefer to make my own. Try making and taste-testing your own recipe at home before canoeing trips.

Other high-energy foods include Fig Newtons, banana chips, breakfast bars, granola bars, dried fruits, Power Bars, oatmeal cookies, and bran muffins. Brownies and candy bars also make good portable snacks. Remember that fats are also part of a daily diet and help make up for the large expenditures of energy. Fats include peanut butter, sunflower seeds, beef jerky, pepperoni or Slim Jims, nuts, cheese, and chocolate.

Water is essential for energy and proper body function, but it's often overlooked. Drink at least 3 to 4 quarts of water per day, especially when paddling long distances and in difficult situations. Powdered drinks like Gatorade or Tang can make plain water more tasty. A sure way to tell whether or not you are drinking sufficient amounts of water is to check your urine. If it is dark, you are dehydrating and must drink more water.

Nalgene bottles are the handiest containers I've found for carrying drinking water. Larger square shape water containers fit neatly into canoes and campsites without falling over as round plastic jugs and containers can. You also should carry water purification tablets and preferably a water purification system. Various systems are available at sporting goods stores. Smaller ones are fine for short trips when you can carry in most of your drinking and cooking water.

Keep in mind that even if brooks and springs look "clean and pure," resist the temptation to drink the water without treating it. Today, acid rain and other pollution and *Giardia* (protozoal cysts) can contaminate even wilderness spring water. We take water for granted, but treating

Easy-to-pack Nalgene bottles and containers are available in various shapes and sizes for all of your food and beverage storage needs.

Meals for the Long Haul

The following are some suggestions for meals on your canoeing adventures:

- **Breakfast:** Instant oatmeal, powdered eggs, poptarts, breakfast squares, hash browns, granola, fresh or dried fruit, hard-boiled eggs, pancakes with fruit or nuts, and even Carnation instant breakfast with powdered milk.

- **Lunch:** Crackers, peanut butter, salami or pepperoni sticks, cheese, Power Bars, cookies, instant soups, sardines, ginger snaps, granola bars, Fig Newtons, nuts, hard candy, beef jerky, fish steaks.

- **Dinner:** Treat yourself nicely with whatever you like. Here's a quick checklist that works well afield. Take with you these staples for cooking: flour, powdered milk, powdered or regular cooking oil, salt, pepper, and Mrs. Dash for flavoring. Also, mince some onions and take along some dehydrated foods such as apples or shrimp.

Cauliflower, onions, peppers, squash, broccoli, zucchini, and cheese are tasty and last well for several days, especially in portable coolers.

water before drinking or cooking is an important habit to cultivate on any outdoor excursion. Jackie Peppe emphasizes taking a water filter on every trip and recommends a Sweetwater or a small Pur. The Pur, she notes, has a mild afterwash of iodine to kill viruses that won't filter out.

STOVE TYPES AND CONSIDERATIONS

It is important to become familiar with your cookstove *before* a trip. Set it up, try it out, and get the feel of cooking with it. Practice lighting your stove, especially if it is a new one, several times before your trip. There is nothing more frustrating and potentially dangerous than being tired, cold, hungry, and wet in the woods without knowing how to operate your stove. Be sure to test any old stove that you haven't used in a while. Long-term storage can cause oxidation and corrosion that clog working parts.

There are many types of camp cooking stoves to choose from, including single-burner white gas, propane, kerosene, or multifuel. Today's camp stoves are remarkably efficient and easy to use. Many are also lightweight and easy to pack for backpacking and canoeing trips. The dwindling supply of firewood along canoeing routes is another good reason to carry a camp stove. In fact, some recreational waterways may restrict or even forbid open fires. Always cook outside, even in the rain; never cook inside any tent. It is dangerous to have an open flame in a tent, especially during the priming process when flame height can be high. Always store stove fuels away from open flames.

Today's camp stoves are remarkably efficient and easy to use.

TYPES OF COOKING FUELS

White gasoline: is a highly refined fuel containing quick-lighting additives and rust inhibitors. It is marketed commercially throughout the U.S. and Canada as Coleman and Blazo fuels. It burns very clean and is less likely to clog tiny burner orifices. White gas is highly volatile and must be kept away from open flames or sparks. Many white gas stoves require *priming*, which is a process of burning a small amount of fuel in a priming pan at the base of the burner until it is well heated. During priming, the fuel is converted from a liquid to a vapor for ignition. Some stoves force fuel into a generator where vaporization takes place. That eliminates the need for the priming process except in very cold temperatures. White gas stoves are generally good performers in all kinds of weather.

Propane gas is often sold in heavy steel cylinders for home barbecue cooking. Smaller cylinders provide the fuel for camp stoves, including single-burner units. Propane is a clean, easy to light fuel; however, as good as propane stoves are, I still prefer butane.

Butane is pressurized in a bottle, which eliminates the need for pumping or priming before lighting a stove. Simply push or screw on a cartridge, light a match, and turn on the valve to produce the flame. Vapor-fed butane cartridges will not vaporize fuel below 32°F at sea level, but few of us go canoeing when weather is that cold.

Advantages of butane are its light weight and simplicity. Some butane stoves weigh just over one pound *with* fuel. Although liquid-fed cartridges will operate in colder weather, they are not recommended for larger groups where you must heat lots of water for cooking, bathing, and cleanup. The butane stove is a good choice for individuals or small groups. You can obtain butane stoves and fuel in most camping supply stores.

Alcohol is an occasional source of stove fuel, but it tends to be an extremely slow way to boil a given quantity of water. Some multifuel stoves will burn alcohol. Boaters often prefer alcohol because it is relatively safe, clean, and evaporates quickly. Supplies may be harder to find, unless you have access to a marina and or boating supply store.

Kerosene is less volatile than white gas, but it is hard to light with a match. Some people prefer kerosene, but the convenience and supply of fuels such as white gas, butane, and propane make kerosene a less likely choice.

Other points to remember: Replace your fuel every season and do not store fuel in a stove or lantern for extended periods of time. Never put your face directly over the burner when lighting or you may singe your eyebrows or worse. Light stoves *outdoors only* and keep spare fuel away from stoves, lanterns, and open flames. Keep fuel containers tightly capped.

CAMPFIRE CONSIDERATIONS

If you will be using a campfire, use the designated fire ring at your campsite if one is available. Have all your wood cut and ready before your begin the meal. If you're using a tarp to protect the cooking area from rain, position it so it won't trap smoke from your cooking fire. When gathering firewood on a canoe trip, stop a mile or so before you get to your campsite and put wood in your canoe. This ensures you will have all you need. In most cases, there will be a scant supply of wood around a regular campsite; it will already have been picked clean by others.

Bring some tinder from home as a back-up plan in case you encounter wet weather. Practice your fire-starting skills at home, before you need them in the wild. Keep in mind that the drier the wood, the less smoke you will have. Driftwood is a good firewood choice. It is easy on the environment and takes little effort to gather. Soft wood will burn hot and fast, but coals will not last very long. Hardwood burns longer and provides a longer-lasting bed of coals for cooking. Veteran wilderness adventurers also advise trying cooking methods at home. Experiment with cook stoves, grills, Dutch ovens, and reflector ovens.

When you pack up to leave, ensure that your fire is completely out before you leave your campsite. Soak the coals with water and stir to expose any hidden embers. Keep soaking and stirring until the fire is dead out and cool to the touch.

While cooking or camping, *never* leave a fire unattended. Winds can come up and blow sparks much farther than you imagine. In re-

If you will be using a campfire, always use the designated fire ring at your campsite, if one is available.

mote areas where there are no campsites with established fire rings, practice "Leave No Trace" standards and double-check to make sure the fire is really out and dead cold before you leave the site.

LIGHT UP THE NIGHT

Naturally, it is important to have light for the night, and several flashlights with extra batteries and bulbs should be in your camping kit. Portable lanterns are an asset, especially in wilderness campsites.

As with stoves, lanterns using different types of fuel are available. Common sense says to use the same type fuel for your stove and lantern. One fuel is convenient and safe and prevents accidently using the wrong fuel in the wrong equipment. If you select a propane lantern, it is possible to run both the stove and lantern off one bulk tank with a series of hoses and fittings.

Portable lanterns are an asset, especially in wilderness campsites.

For lightweight canoeing and camping, your choice should be a small, single-mantle butane or white gas lantern. Backpackers sometimes use a very simple kerosene lantern with a simple wick system and a tank that holds an few ounces of high-grade lamp oil or kerosene. Of course, the simplest lantern is the candle lantern, with its efficient reflector housed in an aluminum or brass cylinder and a glass globe or tube to protect the candle from drafts and rain. Another option is a battery-powered lantern. Many are available, including small pocket-sized versions. The advantage to battery power is you don't need to worry about fuel spills or fires. Although white gas, propane, and butane lanterns provide the brightest light, they can ignite your tent or sleeping bag if tipped over.

Always carry extra mantles—they tend to break easily. And never, never go to sleep with a fueled lantern or stove left on. Accidents do happen, and people do stumble around at night in unfamiliar surroundings. For night light, use your flashlights.

CURIOUS WILD CRITTERS AT CAMP

Creatures and critters in the wild will do what comes naturally, including foraging for food in their habitat where we are camping. However, we should not reinforce an animal's efforts to get our food. Remember, animals generally cannot find what they cannot smell. If you keep a clean camp, you will discourage animal visitors such as ground squirrels, raccoons, skunks, and even bears. Fish guts should be placed far from your camp, on rock, so that scavengers will clean them up quickly, or you can bury waste food and fish parts away from your campsite. Always secure food in animal-proof coolers. Bears can be persistent in trying to open coolers or food containers. In bear areas, it is wise to hang your food high and well, at least 10 feet off the ground and at least 6 feet from the nearest tree trunk.

Bear-proof containers are also a good investment. These containers are odorproof, waterproof, and most importantly, bear- and critter-proof. Smaller food supplies can be well sealed in a food trunk or container. Always keep a trash bag handy and also hang it in a tree. Burn paper trash and keep garbage to a manageable size. Separate cans and bottles for later recycling at home. Before leaving camp, be sure tents are free of food, closed and zippered, and that food is stored properly.

Plan your dishwashing system, using purified water or boiled water. Before preparing each meal, wash your hands with hot soapy water. Wash taste-testing utensils before returning them to the pot.

Keep a checklist of the things you'll need to bring on your camping trip. Knowing you won't be caught short ensures peace of mind once you've arrived at your campsite.

Checklist for Camping

- Lightweight, roomy tents
- Rain fly
- Stakes and poles
- Ground cloths
- Sleeping bags, temperature rated for time of year and comfort
- Mattresses
- Dining fly or tarp with grommets
- Camp ropes, tie-downs
- Camp chairs, butt pads
- Camp pillows
- Lantern with spare mantles and fuel

- Bug repellent and sunscreen lotion
- Candles and candle lantern
- Sven folding hand saw
- Petzol headlamp

Checklist for Cooking and Eating

- Pots with lids, or combo cooking set
- Frying pans with covers
- Eating utensils
- Coffee or tea pot
- Fireplace grill and griddle
- Pot tongs or holders
- Utensil storage bag
- Plates and platter
- Cups (regular and extra collapsible cup)
- Bowls and measuring cup
- Water container for campsite
- Water bottle—one for each person
- Water purification system plus tablets for hiking trips
- Silverware for all individuals
- Kitchen cooking utensils
- Biodegradable soap and pot scrubbers
- Dish towels and paper towels
- Fire starter, spare lighter, waterproof matches
- Pocket lighters for each individual
- Camp stove, funnel, fuel container
- Reflector oven and/or Dutch oven
- Aluminum foil
- Plastic zip-lock bags for food storage
- Trash bags (enough to take out all trash)
- Camp kitchen knife(s)
- Critter-proof food storage box

- Bear bag and ropes
- Camp lantern, extra mantles, fuel
- Extra emergency headlamp or flashlight
- Camera, extra film
- Notebook, pens, pencils
- Plant, animal, bird identification guides
- Folding or other fishing rod, line, lures, flies
- Drop line fishing kit with bobbers, hooks
- Kitchen multipurpose survival tool
- Hot pot tongs

Food Checklist

- Fresh food items
- Breakfast cereals, foods
- Lunch foods—meats, breads, veggies, fruits
- Dinner foods—meats, breads, veggies, fruits, deserts
- Beverages in plastic containers
- Trail and waterway travel snack mixes
- Spices, salt and pepper in container
- Cooking oil, condiments as desired
- Prepared food combos made/packed at home
- Boil-in-bag meals
- Medicines, prescriptions

One of the most satisfying aspects of canoeing is having time to discover the natural wonders that surround us. This little girl takes a moment to quietly observe a tide pool.

CHAPTER 6

Enjoy Natural Discoveries, Wherever You Canoe

Life along waterways is abundant and ever changing. Each time you return to a spot you'll notice something new. Signs of life can be as subtle as a feather in the water or claw scratches on a tree trunk, or tracks along a muddy streambank.

You can best discover the natural wildlife through quiet observation. Sit silently in your canoe for 15 or 20 minutes and you may see a mother duck and her ducklings return from the reeds. A beaver family may resume building or repairing their dam. Birds will begin to call or sing again. As long as their surroundings seem undisturbed and safe, wildlife will go on about their business. Canoeing allows you to glide into animal habitats and soak in the natural wonder that exists when you take time to pause, look, and listen.

Depending upon where you choose to enjoy outdoor adventures, it is helpful to take along pocket-size bird, wildflower, and animal guidebooks to identify what you see.

Bald eagles are making a marvelous comeback. You can occasion-

Be patient. You can best discover natural wildlife through quiet observation.

Paddling past autumn foliage on the Big Fork River, Minnesota.

ally see them along waterways in northern states, soaring above rivers or rapids, especially when fish are spawning. Primarily fish eaters, they'll swoop down to pluck fish right out of the water. In fall and winter, eagles also can be seen as far south as Florida.

Another common predatory bird is the **peregrine falcon.** Once threatened by chemicals in the food chain and water, it is making a steady comeback and can be found in many northern states and along much of the East Coast. It is one of the fastest known flying birds. Diving peregrines have been clocked at over 150 miles per hour. Although they were also called "duck hawks," these birds of prey usually feed on smaller, pigeon- or robin-sized birds.

Kingfishers also favor waterway habitats. These blue and white birds are with a raised crest similar in appearance to bluejays but the male has a rusty band across his chest. Often you'll see kingfishers diving to catch small fish, frogs, and salamanders in their dagger-like bills, or perched in trees along rivers. Curiously, these birds dig long tunnels in riverbanks and make their nests at the end.

Bank swallows also make nests in a hollowed-out chamber at the end of a tunnel in the banks. Unlike kingfishers, which are territorial, bank swallows are social. When one pair finds a suitable riverbank, dozens or hundreds of pairs may join them to dig tunnels and raise their young. Because their favorite foods are mosquitoes, flies, gnats, and other insect pests, swallows can be your ally in controlling insects around your campsite.

Wood ducks have also staged an amazing comeback, thanks to sportsmen's organizations which have erected tens of thousands of wood duck houses along waterways, in swamps, and along the shores of lakes. They are probably the most beautiful of all freshwater ducks. The crested male has shiny feathers of green, blue, and purple, with distinctive white stripes around its face.

Most mammals prefer to sleep by day and forage for food at night. Often, however, you can see some of them at dawn and dusk as you quietly paddle past their habitats.

Raccoons are often curious and are likely to raid a campsite looking for food. These appealing, furry masked bandits prefer to eat along waterways, where they often dunk their food before eating it. Crayfish, toads, frogs, worms, and even birds eggs are their favorites. A mature raccoon can weigh 40 pounds. A mother with several babies is an amusing sight. Look for their footprints along shorelines.

Beavers were the big money makers for the fur trappers that first canoed across America's frontiers. They are the largest rodents in North America, growing up to 75 pounds or more. Their flat tail is covered with scales and is used as a rudder when swimming. It also serves as a tool when beavers make their lodge homes and dams.

Look along shores for poplar and willow trees that have been cut down by the beavers' sharp teeth. Often they will ignore quiet canoeists as they go about their busy work, cutting saplings, making dams, and carrying tree pieces to store in their lodges as winter food. If you disturb them, they'll respond with a resounding slap of their flat tail on the water to warn their fellow beavers, then dive and swim quickly away to safety.

In contrast to the busy beavers who always seem to be working, **river otters** are one of the most playful of river dwellers. Most animals spend their days looking for food. Otters take time to play. You may see them sliding down a muddy or grassy riverbank, just for fun. Unlike most small mammals, otters are active during daylight. Fish are the otters' main food item, so you also may see them slicing through the water in hot pursuit. With torpedo-shaped bodies propelled by webbed feet, otters are fast enough to capture speedy trout, but slower fish, frogs, crayfish, and insects make up the bulk of their diet.

Beavers were busy here building this lodge for shelter and food storage.

The otter—one of the most playful of river dwellers.

Moose are one of the most popular wilderness attractions in Maine and other northern states. With giant antlers, a bull moose is a marvelous sight, belly deep at lakeside, ducking its head to pull up tasty aquatic weeds and plants. Often you'll see a cow and calf, eating peacefully without even bothering to look at you as you paddle past.

Though this moose is clearly on the lookout, you'll often see a moose eating peacefully, undisturbed as you paddle quietly past.

A fawn resting on a grassy bank.

Deer are one of the most common sights along waterways, providing there are pastures and meadows where they can find their favorite foods.

Although you may not realize it, along every stream and lake shore, and around your campground sites, you're being watched. The fact is, there may be more pairs of eyes watching you at night than you imagine. Many wild creatures are nocturnal. They rest by day and come out at night to forage for food, including your food if you don't secure it properly.

Come dawn, you'll often find curious footprints around your camp (see pages 84–85), in the mud and sand at water's edge. Deer, raccoons, opossums, skunks, and even porcupines may have visited you while you slept.

Casting Animal Tracks

Naturally, you should leave no footprints of your own when canoeing and camping, or take any "souvenirs" home, but casting animal tracks is a way you can collect mementos of the animal visits during your canoeing adventures. It is a fun hobby for children, too. All you need to make casts is:

* 1 pound of plaster of Paris
* Cardboard strips

Continued

- Sticks
- A mixing pot or bucket
- Water to mix the casting material

Look for the clearest track you can find. The best ones will be in mud, moist sand, or fine gravel. Follow directions on the box of plaster of Paris to mix a smooth, slightly runny paste.

Take a cardboard strip (cut from shirt cardboard or pads of lined paper, or old notebook covers). Cut 2-inch wide strips about 10 inches long.

Make a circle of this cardboard strip that will enclose the entire track. Then paperclip the ends together. Gently press the cardboard into the soil around the track. Be careful that you don't disturb the track, especially in sandy or gravelly soils.

Next, pour the plaster of Paris mix into all parts of the track, starting with the finer parts, such as toenail marks. Then, cover the track completely to an thickness of 1 inch, for a deer track, or less, for small chipmunk or squirrel tracks.

Spread the paste ½ inch or more beyond the limits of the track to the cardboard that will hold it in place.

Then, place several reinforcing sticks, each about half the size of a pencil, into the surface of the paste, making a criss-

Top: Mix Plaster of Paris in a plastic container and pour into the cardbord "mold" you place around the animal track.
Bottom: Let the plaster dry for 20-30 minutes and then wipe or brush away any dirt or debris from the cast of the animal track.

cross as reinforcement. You can use coffee stirring sticks, cut to size. Add a bit more paste to cover the sticks. When the plaster sets, these sticks will reinforce the cast and help prevent cracking or breaking.

Let the plaster set and do not disturb the track while the plaster sets firmly. This should take 20 to 30 minutes.

Then, carefully pick up the cast so you don't break any part of it. Then, brush or wash away any debris that still clings to it.

This is actually a positive (raised) impression of the track. To make a negative imprint, as the tracks appear in nature, make a circle of cardboard around the positive cast and tape or paperclip the edges together. You can do this at home or school.

Mix more plaster. Then, coat the raised (positive) print with a thin coat of Vaseline. Next, pour the plaster on top and allow it to harden. When it is well set, in 20 to 30 minutes, carefully remove the positive mold and wipe it clean. You'll now have both a negative and positive animal track for your collections.

Like to have more fun? You can surprise friends and neighbors by using the positive track mold early morning or late evening to make "animal" tracks in a friend's backyard. Won't your friends be surprised when they discover these tracks of a big deer or even a giant moose that seems to have visited their yard!

Continued

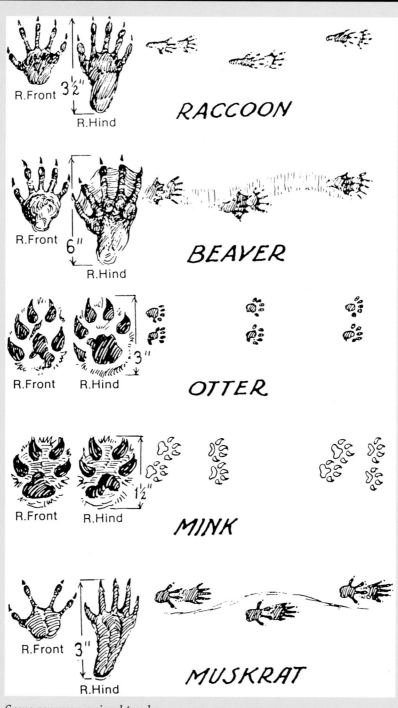

Some common animal tracks.

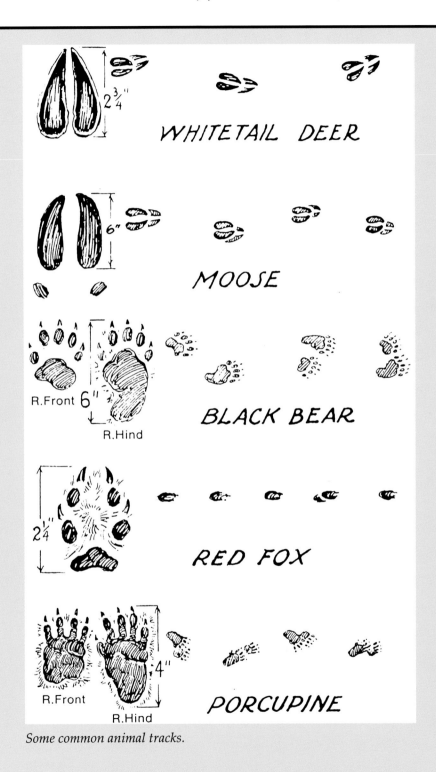

Some common animal tracks.

FISHING FOR SUPER SUPPERS

Fishing for a fresh, tasty wilderness supper is one of the simplest and cheapest sports ever conceived. Except for a hook and line, all you need is a little patience and an understanding of the wheres and whys of cold-water fish, plus a fishing license, of course. You may prefer fancy fishing gear, but a hand line and hook will do as well.

Ask any fisherman what the most popular, tastiest fish is in rivers and lakes and he'll most likely say *trout*. Depending on what part of the country you canoe, trout could include rainbows, steelheads, cutthroats, Dolly Vardens, common brook, and brown trout. Most trout spend their entire lives in cool, flowing rivers and streams. Some types thrive in lakes. A packable fly rod and reel with flies is handy if you like trout. Trout also feed on worms, crickets, and other insects you can catch along the shore or around your campsite.

Because many other fish are often more abundant, a simple casting rod and reel does double duty. One or two hand lines with bobbers and hooks are more easily stored and perform adequately when fishing from a canoe or shore. My fisherman son recalls how he watched a youngster with a hand line and worms outfish several adults equipped with the best fishing gear money could buy. Part of the fun is watching to see what fish are eating and matching the bait to the natural food of the day.

Catfish are becoming popular as people realize how tasty they are. They are bottom feeders, identified by the whiskerlike spines around their mouths, and are scaleless. Beware the fins when unhooking and handling. The spines on fins can sting, so handle carefully.

Large- and smallmouth **bass** are common in most lakes and may reach 3 to 5 pounds. Worms, small frogs, minnows, and artificial lures are the best baits. Chain pickerel also inhabit many ponds and lakes. They too often respond to lures or live bait.

Sunfish, bluegills, rock bass, and **perch** are other common freshwater fish. Like chain pickerel, these tend to be bonier than trout, bass, or catfish; however, all are delicious, especially if cleaned and cooked within an hour or so of catching them.

There are two basic, distinctly different ways to catch fish with live bait; *float fishing* and *drift fishing*. For float fishing choose a calm, slow-moving area of the stream. Deep pools below rapids or waterfalls are great spots. Estimate the depth of the water and attach your float on the line almost that depth from the hook. The float will hold your bait off the bottom so fish can see it. It will also wiggle or bob and even get pulled under water when a fish bites. Watch it carefully.

In drift fishing there is no bobber to indicate that a fish is biting. You must continually watch the line. If it tightens or veers to one side or another, you have a fish. That's the time to give the line a sharp pull to set the hook so the fish can't swallow it or spit it out.

Timing is important. Setting the hook too soon could pull the bait and hook out of a fish's mouth. When a fish picks up a bit of food, it usually moves the morsel around in its mouth before swallowing it. Only when the fish begins to move away with the bait should you try to set the hook. Pull up sharply on the pole or line and the hook should set itself in the fish's lip. Keep some tension on the line as you pull it in. Any slack will allow the fish a chance to shake the hook loose, and away swims your supper.

There are many useful how-to books about fishing. You can spend a fortune on fishing equipment. However, one fact remains: in the wilderness, rivers and lakes are seldom overfished. A simple rod and reel or drop line is often fully adequate to catch yourself, family, and friends a tasty meal.

Once you've caught your share of fish for the day, now comes the messy part. You must prepare them for cooking and eating. The easiest way is to spread some paper and lay the fish on its back. Make a shallow cut in a circle around the vent and then cut towards the head. Next, cut through the backbone and, using the severed head as a handle, pull the entrails from the body cavity. All the major organs should stay together, and you can roll them up and bury them in a cat hole, just as you would with other waste. Wash the body cavity and you're ready to cook. Most people prefer to remove the scales and skin before cooking. By running warm water over the body for several minutes, you can peel them off easily in one piece.

Fish seem to taste best if they are cleaned and cooked as soon as possible. Perhaps it also is the ambiance of the setting, around a cookstove or campfire in your own discovered piece of majestic wilderness. *Bon appetit.*

This man takes a break from paddling to fish for supper.

Environmental stewardship is a practice that's worth passing along to everyone. Learning skills and making decisions based on an outdoor ethic benefits ecosystems now and helps conserve the environment for future generations.

CHAPTER
7

Environmental Stewardship: Leave No Trace

People who really care about preserving, protecting, and enjoying the great outdoors have adopted the "Leave No Trace" motto as their Golden Rule. This code clearly expresses the need for environmental stewardship of this planet we all share and wish to leave as unspoiled as possible for future generations. As millions more venture further afield and afloat, it makes sense to leave the wilderness in the same condition, or better, than we found it. That's a legacy worth passing along here and to everyone who shares a common bond for outdoor adventure.

Every canoeist can minimize his or her impact on the land and waterways. Learning skills and making decisions based on an outdoor ethics program does conserve the environment and ecosystems. Leave No Trace is a basic philosophy shared by the instructors at the L.L. Bean Outdoor Discovery School. It also is the outdoor adventure philosophy shared by leaders at the American Canoeing Association, Boy Scouts and Girl Scouts of America, and every other responsible outdoor group.

Because environmental stewardship is so important today, a composite Leave No Trace guideline program is included in this book. The following key guideposts include the best elements of several programs developed by various organizations.

SEVEN LEAVE-NO-TRACE GUIDEPOST PRINCIPLES

1. **Plan Ahead and Prepare Properly.** Advance planning is the first and easiest step to protect and preserve the wilderness. Repack food supplies to minimize container trash. Always plan to take plastic garbage and smaller plastic bags so you can carry out any excess food and debris, including any mess left by previous inconsiderate campers. Plan to use portable cookstoves, to avoid the need for cutting firewood or making unnecessary campfires.

   Proper planning ensures low-risk adventures. Locate designated campsites and allow enough paddling time to reach your daily destination. Allow for varying wind, water, and weather conditions. All of this planning helps you avoid making unnecessary stops, which could mean creating new campsites in wilderness areas.

2. **Avoid Damage to Ecosystems.** Damage to land and waterways occurs when visitors trample vegetable or communities of organisms beyond recovery. Care in landing, launching, or portaging is essential to protect shorelines. So is careful choice and use of rest stop areas and overnight campsites. In high-use areas, you should concentrate your activities in areas where vegetation is already absent. You can minimize resource damage by using existing trails and designated or existing campsites.

Care in landing, launching, or portaging is essential to protect shorelines. Watch your step!

That includes using the same campfire sites, or better yet, using portable cookstoves rather than campfires.

In remote wilderness areas, you should spread out. Take different paths to avoid making new trails that cause erosion. Disperse tents and cooking activities. Move your camp daily to avoid creating permanent campsites. It is best to choose the most durable surfaces such as rock, gravel, and dry grasses to avoid damaging tender plants.

Never dig tent trenches, hammer nails in trees, or hack at the bark to leave trail markers. In wilderness areas, replace any rocks or branches you cleared for a sleeping spot. In high-traffic areas, clean the area well and dismantle appropriate things such as multiple fire rings, manmade seats, benches, or other trappings of civilization.

3. **Pack It In, Pack It Out.** This step is one of the keys to Leave No Trace camping. Carefully plan meals and repack foods before embarking to eliminate excessive cans, bottles, cardboard packages, plastic containers and leftover food. You'll save weight and space and eliminate trash to carry out. Boil-in-a-bag type meals and trail mixes are especially useful.

Body wastes require special attention. Always dig *cat holes*. Use a metal garden trowel to cut a piece of sod 5 to 6 inches in diameter and

"Pack it in, pack it out." This family will be sure to take all of their trash with them when they go.

remove it. Then dig cat holes 6 to 8 inches deep and at least 200 feet from water, trails, and campsites. Use toilet paper sparingly. Then bury waste with paper and replace the "sod" or piece of top ground.

Avoid contamination of natural water sources by straining food particles from dishwater. Disperse the wastewater 200 feet or more away from any natural water source.

Finally, pack out any refuse in plastic bags, so you truly leave no trace at any campsite or shoreline. The wild creatures and canoeists who travel there in the future will greatly appreciate your efforts to preserve the natural environment without traces of civilization.

4. **Leave What You Find Behind.** Every outdoor adventurer has a sense of discovery. Many are tempted to take a piece of memorabilia home. Don't! Leave attractive stones or rocks, flowers, plants, animals, and especially any archeological artifacts and other objects you find where you discovered them. Fact is, it is usually illegal to remove artifacts and rare or endangered flowers and plants. Leave them be. Wild plants and animals need their own unique ecosystem to survive and reproduce.

5. **Minimize Use of Campsites.** You may find many areas have been damaged or degraded by overuse of fires and picking or cutting of firewood. If possible, always pack in your own lightweight stoves. They eliminate the need for fires and cutting down wood and don't require cleanup. Instead of building a campfire, plan to enjoy the evening by candle or gas lantern light.

If you do build a fire, use the existing campfire ring at the campsite. Use dead wood for a fire and burn all wood to ash. Remove all unburned trash from the fire ring—be sure it is "dead" cold with all sparks gone. Finally, bury cold ashes to leave the campfire spot neater than you found it. Naturally, elect not to use a campfire where wood is scarce, during periods when risk of forest fires is high, or whenever possible, especially in wilderness areas.

6. **Respect Wild Critters and Creatures.** Wild animals of all sizes can be disturbed in their natural habitats, especially in wilderness areas where they are unaccustomed to human visits. Avoid quick movements and loud noises. Carry binoculars and telephoto camera lenses to observe birds and animals from a distance. Some

Use dead wood for fires and burn all wood to ash. Make sure the ashes are cold and bury them before you go. Leave your campsite neater than you found it.

animals can be troublesome when disturbed, especially during breeding, nesting, and birthing seasons. Moose can stumble into your camp. Bears like to forage for food. Skunks can be curious and smelly when frightened.

Always store food securely and keep garbage and food scraps sealed away. Some human foods are harmful to wild critters, which is why it is important to pack out all excess food, cooked or not. Wild animals and birds should be left to be wild, in the wild.

7. **Respect Your Fellow Canoeists.** Always obtain permission from landowners or appropriate agencies, get permits if required, including fire permits, and observe the rules of the waterway wherever you canoe. Travel and camp in small groups in wilderness areas. Leave radios and tape recorders home.

   Select campsites away from other groups to preserve their privacy and protect your own. Camp quietly and demonstrate your knowledge and concern for Leave No Trace outdoor etiquette. Offer to help others clean up a campground. Novices often learn by seeing good outdoor manners demonstrated. Wear clothing and gear that blend with the environment. You'll blend in better to see the living wonders of nature and feel more naturally at home.

The Boy Scouts of America have an effective, ongoing Leave No Trace program for leaders and scouts. They've been promoting it for years. They deserve a salute for it and often are glad to discuss and share their program with others in their communities. Leaders who pass an advanced course of requirement qualify as "Masters of Leave No Trace." Those that learn pass it on, training other leaders and scouts.

Youth and adults who participate in unit-based Leave No Trace training are eligible for the BSA's Leave No Trace Awareness award. To qualify, leaders and advisors must explain the principles of Leave No Trace. On three separate camping or backpacking trips they must demonstrate and practice the LNT principles. They also must share with another Scout leader their understanding and knowledge of the Camping and Environmental Science merit badge requirements, actively assist a scout in planning, organizing, and leading a service project related to that theme, assist a minimum of three scouts in earning the LNT Awareness Award and plan and conduct a LNT session for Scouts, Scouters, Advisors or an interested group outside of Scouting.

Details about the LNT program are available by contacting your local Boy Scouts of America troops. As you plan your next canoeing adventure, read this chapter again. You too can be a pioneer in promoting this vital and sound ideal. Leave No Trace deserves to be every canoeist's personal goal.

Remember, costly mistakes made while canoeing and camping can be avoided if plans are carefully worked out among your group **before** *you get underway.*

CHAPTER 8

Canoeing Safe, Sane, and Secure

In addition to wearing PFDs, the most important canoeing and water safety consideration, there are other points to keep in mind to canoe safe, sane, and secure. Some of these points may seem so basic and simple that we tend to overlook or neglect them, which is all the more reason to reiterate them here.

CANOE SAFE AND SANE POINTS

Common sense is a big asset in life and in canoeing. Often we get ourselves in trouble when we neglect common sense or discount our gut instincts.

Remember, you alone are responsible for your own safety.

The best rescue is no rescue. Never paddle any place you are not comfortable swimming. Always paddle with people who agree to help you if you are in trouble. Practice self-rescue techniques before your trip and whenever you capsize.

If you do capsize, follow these rescue procedures: Hang on to your equipment with one hand. Check yourself, your partner, and your equipment, in that order. Get upstream of your boat with your feet near the water surface so the river current doesn't push the canoe and you downstream. Never stand in moving water that is deeper than your knees.

In fast-moving water with many rocks, float on your back while hanging onto your equipment with one hand. If you are right-handed, hold the canoe with your left and backstroke towards an eddy or shore with your right hand. Do the reverse with your hands if you are left-handed. Once the water smooths out a bit, swim toward shore or an eddy aggressively. For example, if you are swimming to river right, stroke with your right arm while looking downstream for hazards.

Although it is important to help rescue other people in a capsize situation, remember that one-third of all people who drown in whitewater rescues are the rescuers. Don't panic or overreact. Ask yourself whether you are doing a rescue or a body recovery. If you are trying to rescue a victim, speed is important.

Use common sense in every rescue effort. Throw bags and throw ropes are the best way to rescue people. Extending paddles, long branches of trees or clothes tied together are more advisable methods than entering the water yourself. Only as a last resort should you enter the water yourself, and you should be wearing a PFD.

Carry a throw bag in every boat and stuff all of them yourself so you know they are right and ready. Learn, understand and practice proper use of your throw rope. Throw ropes should be 50 to 75 feet long and of ⅜ to ½ inch in diameter, brightly colored, and used *only* for rescues. Never put them to other uses or they won't be there when you may need them in an emergency situation.

DRINK WATER TO PADDLE BETTER

Pure water, and lots of it, is another basic but often overlooked key factor on canoeing trips, especially when expending lots of energy paddling against currents, winds, and whitecaps. No matter what the air temperature, strenuous exercise causes water loss through perspiration and respiration. When water consumption does not match our body's increased needs, adverse side effects can occur. Two of the earliest signs of dehydration are headaches and dark, concentrated urine. Dehydration also causes fatigue, irritability, poor thinking, thirst, and dizziness. If you don't address the situation, you can even be faced with changes in mental awareness, loss of balance, and lowered blood volume.

You should drink at least 1 quart of water before starting on a trip and take several quarts of water with you to drink during the day. Then, drink another quart with your evening meal. Some people like to mix flavoring with water for variety. Add your favorite powdered beverage mixes to your food checklist. However, try to avoid taking in too much caffeine. Caffeine in tea, coffee, and some sodas is a diuretic that stimulates kidneys to increase urinary output. Alcohol also increases urine production and fluid loss. Too many caffeineated beverages will defeat the purpose of rehydration.

COLD WATER AND WEATHER

Waterways are usually less crowded in early spring and late fall, but the weather and water can be colder than you expect. Hypothermia, especially if you end up in the water, can be a serious problem. Early warning signs of hypothermia are sensation of cold, especially in the chest area, cold hands and feet, and possible numbness and uncontrollable shivering. These early warning signs tell you that your body is having trouble keeping warm. If you don't take steps to reduce or eliminate the cold stress, accidental hypothermia can result. Get ashore, dry out thoroughly at a safely made campfire, change clothes, and dry those that became wet. Take time to check all other gear, dry it out, and rest after any accident until you have fully regained your proper focus. Then, recheck all safety considerations before paddling on. Naturally, if a serious emergency occurs it is important to call, signal, or attempt to get appropriate help or rescue aid.

Proper layering of clothing so you can take off clothes during vigorous exercise and add on layers as needed is the basic way to stay warm and comfortable and avoid cold weather problems.

WEATHER SIGNS AND SIGNALS

Always check weather reports before you leave for a day or longer trip. Because weather can change so rapidly, even professionals have difficulty predicting changes. It helps to take along a weather radio and to check the weather reports periodically.

Most weather systems move from west to east, so keep a weather eye focused to the west. Wind shifts generally indicate changing weather conditions. Winds are caused by changing barometric pressure and a drop in barometric pressure indicates bad weather is coming.

Clouds can provide a guide to changing weather. Flat, *stratus* clouds are normally associated with stable air. Puffy, *cumulus* clouds indicate unstable air. The greater the vertical development of the clouds, the greater their instability. Thunderstorm clouds have the greatest vertical development and tell you weather may become violent.

The U.S. Government has several excellent flyers that show types of clouds and provide details about their meaning and the weather they foretell.

Waves are created by blowing wind. The stronger the wind and the longer and farther it blows, the larger the waves. Birds and animals can also signal coming storms. If birds and animals have taken to protective cover, take a tip from their behavior. Instinct tells them many things about the natural environment that we may overlook. If you should spot any of these weather danger signals, canoe closer to shore and always put ashore to wait out any storm.

WHEN LIGHTNING STRIKES

Lightning is responsible for about 100 deaths and 300 injuries annually. Activity around water accounts for 40 percent of these deaths. More canoeists die of lightning strikes than any other cause. When a lightning storm threatens, use common sense precautions.

If you are on the water when a storm approaches, get close to shore and find a safe place to get off the water as soon as possible before the storm hits your area. It is best to assume a protected position when the storm hits. A recommended protected position is to squat or sit on an insulative pad, a sleeping pad, or your PFD, with your feet close to your body and your hands in your lap or around your knees. The fewer points of contact with the ground and the closer these points of contact are to each other, the safer the position. The danger of lightning is not only being struck directly, but also exposure to ground currents from a nearby strike. They can pass through the body and vital organs.

Don't sit under or against a tree. Woodlands are generally a safe place to be, but avoid tall trees and sit *between* trees rather than near or under one. Never lean against a tree or any other object.

If you feel a change of sensation or a lot of static electricity in the air, drop to a protected position. That could be the only warning you get before a nearby lightning strike. Remember that lightning often stuns rather than kills and cardiac arrest can occur. It pays to take basic First Aid courses, including CPR, to prepare yourself for wilderness trips and any emergency situations you may face. The American Red Cross, local Fire and Rescue departments, and Adult Education programs provide valuable classes in most communities.

LOST PERSON BASICS

National statistics show that 50 percent of people who become lost die within 24 hours. The missing person can be expected to be found in a relatively small area when first lost, but as time passes he or she may wander much farther afield, especially if disoriented. An ounce of prevention is worth a pound of cure, especially when you become a wilderness explorer. Learning basic First Aid is one step. Learning map reading and compass use is another.

Every person in your group should be equipped with a compass and know how to use it.

Before starting on your journey, it is wise to review the waterway route with all participants and compare maps and compass bearings. Make sure you have safety equipment, including a weather radio, signal devices, and other necessary items for longer periods in the wild. You'll find a helpful checklist of safety equipment at the end of this chapter.

If you discover you have a lost person, go immediately to the last known point where that person was seen and signal by voice, whistle, foghorn, or whatever system you worked out *in advance*. Alert other members of your party that a person seems to have become lost. Insist that they stay together.

If immediate signaling does not get a response, then you must consider a longer and more thorough search. This requires consideration of the weather, time of day, terrain ashore, and the age and physical state of the lost person. Once you have assessed the situation, it is imperative that a diligent, common-sense effort be made to locate the lost person, without losing any others of your party in the effort. It may be necessary to call or go for help from the warden or ranger service covering that area. They are trained for rescues.

It's most important to train yourself, your family, and fellow explorers in the key steps they should take if they become lost. Most people, when placed in a survival situation, make a conscious decision within the first 6 hours as to whether or not they will live or die. It's important therefore not to panic. Once you realize that you are lost and must spend an unplanned night in the woods, STOP. That stands for Stop, Think, Organize, Plan. Take it easy and assure yourself that you will be okay.

Pause and think. If you are lost, how did you get to that spot? How long have you been in the woods separated from others in your party, or by yourself, if you are on an individual trip. How long has it been since you knew where you were? Look at the topographic map that you should have tucked in a pocket before you ever ventured afield from your waterway. Are there any key features? In which direction and how far away is the nearest road?

If you become injured, use your First Aid training and knowledge to repair yourself as best you can. Then, don't overtax your body by too pushing yourself too hard.

Plan. You will need shelter, water, fire, and food, in that order. Think of the most efficient way to get all these things. Are you carrying a tent, tarp, or space blanket? If not, use materials available to erect a shelter. This could be a lean-to of branches or a bark shelter. Be sure to insulate yourself from the ground, using boughs, leaves, or dry debris.

Ration your food and water. If there are water sources where you are, filter or treat the water with iodine or purification tablets, or boil the water. If you are unable to treat water, drink it anyway. If you become dehydrated, your body functions less efficiently and your judgement can be impaired. Symptoms of water-borne illness take about a week to be felt and such illness is rarely fatal. Without water, however, you are unlikely to survive more than two or three days and your functioning will be severely impaired each day you are inadequately hydrated.

Fire will help you maintain body temperature and kill bacteria in water and food. Fire gave the cave man comfort. It also can warm your spirits and fuel your survival instincts. Fires can be started with flint and steel or Indian skill style, by twirling hand drill in tinder, but not without knowledge and practice. Always carry a pocket lighter or weatherproof matches (or both) and know how to find good tinder to build a fire, even in wet conditions.

Food will help your energy level but you can actually survive without it for many days, if you have water. Conserve your energy. Trying to capture animals for food requires expending more time and energy it is usually worth. Many plants have great nutritional value, but others are poisonous. It always pays to learn about native plants to live off the land if required. Learn to identify which berries and nuts are safe to eat. Cattails offer nourishment, as the North American Indians long knew.

Once you have made your rudimentary shelter, are adequately hydrated, and are using enough energy to keep warm or have a fire, slow down. Don't wander aimlessly. Wandering further afield without a plan is foolish. It makes a search party's job harder.

Assess your situation again. Did you leave your float plan and time away schedule with a responsible person who will realize they should try to find you if you don't return on schedule to check in?

Review your map and compass. Reorient yourself. Stay in one place with a fire going. You can make the fire smokier by adding moist wood to it, which will provide a signal for people to find you.

These points aren't intended as more than basic considerations. Reading them, you'll realize that taking map and compass courses, learning basic First Aid, and perhaps also some wilderness survival skills can be as important as knowing how best to paddle a canoe.

Here's a checklist of key items to take on your trip. Those marked with an asterisk (*) should always be in the pockets or pack of each individual for reference and use in emergencies. You can add to this basic list or select from it as you prefer.

Safety Supply Checklist

- Basic field First Aid kit or items as indicated
- 1 roll 1-inch adhesive gauze
- 2 4 × 4 gauze pads
- 1 large dressing
- 1 3-inch elastic bandage
- 5 or more Bandaids
- 1 blister pad
- Several diaper or large safety pins
- Pair of splinter tweezers
- Emergency flashlight*
- Small metal mirror for signaling*
- Multiblade pocket knife*
- Pocket lighter and/or waterproof matches*
- Tube of iodine or antiseptic
- Tube of sunblock/sunscreen
- Tylenol, Ibuprofen, or similar pain pills
- Small tube of liquid soap

Other important safety and emergency items:

- Hand compass*
- Topo map of area
- Insect repellent
- Whistle or signaling device*
- Personal water bottle*
- Water purification tablets
- Extra set of waterproof matches or lighter

Canoe classes and excursions can help paddlers of all ages hone their skills.

CHAPTER
9

Canoeing Classes and Excursions for Beginners to Advanced

appily, many canoeing classes, courses, and competitions are offered around the country. L.L. Bean has been conducting Outdoor Discovery classes for years, covering many topics. So has the American Canoe Association. So do many local and area outfitters today.

L.L. BEAN OUTDOOR DISCOVERY SCHOOL

For many years, L.L. Bean has been offering classes, short courses and exciting canoeing adventures on some of Maine's most dramatic canoeing lakes and rivers. Every year, expert canoeists provide these Outdoor Discovery School programs for beginners and intermediate and advanced canoeing enthusiasts.

Learn to Paddle Solo in Your Canoe

This course is designed to give you the skills you need to paddle a canoe efficiently by yourself. You'll focus on paddling straight, maneuvering, and stopping. You'll also learn easy ways to carry your canoe to the water, trim it for a variety of wind conditions, and control your canoe with confidence. This course usually runs from early June through August.

Honing Your Tandem Canoe Skills

If you paddle but have never had any formal instruction, this class will help you enjoy your canoeing experiences more and save you energy on your next adventure afloat. Working as a team with your partner, you'll learn how to keep your canoe on a straight path by combining various paddle strokes. You'll learn how to maneuver the canoe with minimal effort. Equally important, you'll gain increased efficiency to get more hours of enjoyment from your paddling trips. This class is designed for individuals and you will be paired with another person of similar skills. This course usually runs from June through August.

Quick-start Your Canoe

This class can teach you to become more proficient at paddling. You get to practice refining your strokes in both solo and tandem style to become a more competent and confident paddler. In this course you'll also learn great tips for loading and cartopping a canoe, plus the right knots to keep it secure. This class is usually offered from June through early September.

Freestyle Canoe Solo

This is a course to help you learn how to make your canoe dance across the water. This is an advanced paddler's workshop to help you understand the hydrodynamics of your canoe and how to use its built-in qualities to enhance boat performance. Instructors guide you step-by-step through the skills you'll need to effect 180-degree turns, as well as slide slips and diagonal movement through the water, plus moving both forward and in reverse with paddle placement on both the on- and off-side of the canoe. From this course, you'll achieve the ultimate in canoe control. This course is given July through September. Basic canoeing experience is a prerequisite.

Freestyle Canoe Tandem

Canoes have symmetry that allows all maneuvers to be done equally effectively traveling forward and backward, on-side as well as off-side. You'll learn the building blocks needed for the exacting boat control demanded in freestyle paddling.

This is the ultimate in tandem canoe handling. You and your partner will become better and more efficient tandem canoeists. You can bring a friend or come alone and be paired with a canoe mate. Given July through September.

Outdoor Discover School canoeing instructor Jackie Peppe teaches and canoes whenever she can.

Moving Water Workshop for the Tandem Canoeist

Many canoe trips include stretches of white water. In this advanced class, you will learn to control and maneuver your boat in moving water. You'll get to understand and use the river currents for eddy turns, peel-outs, and ferries. Plus, you'll learn rescues for paddlers and boats. Your stokes and confidence will improve after three days on water of differing degrees of difficulty. Given in July and August. Prerequisites include basic courses or equivalent experience.

Kids' Canoe Lessons

Children love canoeing and usually learn the basics fast. L.L. Bean instructors encourage all youngsters to learn to enjoy the outdoors and have fun while attending Outdoor Discovery Schools. Safe, hands-on learning and exciting methods of teaching are two key ingredients that make these courses lively, informative, and practical. Under a watchful eye, kids become familiar with boating safety and paddling etiquette.

Canoeing Day Trips

Half the fun of canoeing is discovering what can't be seen from shore. In this course kids learn to paddle a canoe safely while looking for wildlife along the shoreline. They'll look for birds, plants, and bugs and learn about the environment and protecting it too.

Parent and Child Canoe Overnight

Listening to loons, participants will set up base camp on the shore of Crescent Lake. They'll learn to pitch tents, cook meals, and acquire many other important outdoor skills. Learning to paddle together, parent and child will also enjoy games designed to reinforce canoeing and outdoor skills. On the second day, time is available for lunch and exploring the shoreline by canoe to discover birds, wildlife, and other natural wonders.

Map and Compass, Level I

Leon Leonwood Bean, the founder of L.L. Bean, once wrote, "The best compass in the world is useless if you do not know how to use it." No matter what your outdoor interest—canoeing, camping, or hiking—knowing how to use a map and compass in the field will increase your confidence. Map and Compass Level I is a three-hour indoor class that introduces the fundamentals of topographic map reading. You will learn to identify map features, determine distances, and figure elevations. After learning the parts of a compass, you will learn to orient a map, plot courses, and take bearings.

Map and Compass Level II

If you already know how to use a compass, this may be a more appropriate class. This day-long course is a comprehensive lesson on getting around the outdoors and on waterways. You will review the basics, then spend the afternoon using practical applications of map and compass skills in everyday situations; following a bearing through thick woods, finding your position by triangulating, boxing around obstacles, and orienting yourself in the field. By the end of the day, you'll be able to successfully plot a course on a map and follow it on the trail.

COURSES IN MEDICINE FOR THE OUTDOORS

As wilderness adventure becomes increasingly popular, it pays to remember that there is no 911 emergency service to call in the wilderness. Some basic wilderness First Aid training can be very useful. The Outdoor Discovery School offers several courses taught by professional instructors from the Wilderness Medical Associates. Focusing on medical emergencies you might encounter in the outdoors, the courses include lecture time, hands-on practice, and simulated emergencies.

Wilderness First Aid

This is a basic course designed to teach you how to handle medical emergencies when you are miles from assistance. You'll learn how to assess injuries, stabilize trauma, and perform wilderness rescues. This workshop provides a solid foundation for trip leaders, guides, instructors, and other outdoor enthusiasts who will be involved in remote area trips.

Wilderness First Aid for Families

This is an eight-hour introductory class for kids 12 and up and their families. It provides information to think your way through and effectively respond to a crisis. By role-playing some common medical emergencies your family might encounter in the outdoors, you will learn to assess the victim and prepare for a rescue. The day is composed of lectures, demonstrations, and lots of hands-on practice for all.

Wilderness Advanced First Aid

This is a four-day course focusing on the fundamentals of First Aid assistance in remote areas. Participants who successfully complete the exam will be certified to administer Wilderness Advanced First Aid.

The Outdoor Discovery School also offers more advanced and longer courses for those who will be taking longer trips into remote areas and want to have greater knowledge for the safety of their families and friends who also will be spending more time in wilderness areas.

OUTDOOR DISCOVERY SCHOOL CANOE TRIPS AFLOAT

A variety of different trips are available every year, guided by Outdoor Discovery School experts. The following are some examples:

Day Tripping in a Canoe

A relaxing paddle down one of the favorite local Maine rivers. Throughout the day, you have ample opportunity to practice your canoeing skills and learn new ones. You'll pick up tips for fun canoe trips and share the day with other enthusiasts. This trip includes a stop along the way for picnic lunch. Given in July and August.

Moose River Canoe Trip

You'll enjoy a classic four-day trip linking the Moose River and Attean and Holeb Ponds. On this adventure, you'll paddle the winding Moose River through quiet and quick water and tent in the heart of moose country. You'll learn to pack efficiently for the short portages that break up each day and to use a map and compass. In addition, you'll learn to set a Leave-No-Trace campsite and enjoy cooking nutritious meals.

Crossing remote ponds, you'll travel back in time to the days of early traders and explorers when time was measured by the changing seasons. On the last day, you may also climb Sally Mountain for a panoramic view of the wild waterway you've paddled. Given during July.

Canoeing the West Branch of the Penobscot

This exciting trip with instructors and Registered Maine Guides is one of Maine's classic canoeing experiences. The Penobscot was formerly used as a major route for the logging industry. Today, this waterway remains a popular corridor for recreational boaters and fishermen. You'll spend six days exploring and paddling the same route that Thoreau used on his way to Chesuncook Lake. Given in August.

Five-Day Allagash Canoe Trip from Round Pond

Registered Maine Guides and Outdoor Discovery School instructors guide you on a leisurely trip down the historic Allagash River. Designated as a National Scenic Waterway, it has some of the most remote wilderness areas, abundant with wildlife and breathtaking scenery. Your paddling skills will improve as you travel up to 12 miles each day. Camping along the riverbanks, you'll learn time-tested wilderness skills to help you plan trips of your own. Given each summer.

Seven-Day Allagash Canoe Trip from Umsaskis Lake

This extended trip along the fabled Allagash Waterway gives you two more days of outdoor adventures. For both the five- and seven-day trips, canoeing experience is preferred. Given each summer.

Women's Only Canoe Trips

These trips are guided by Outdoor Discovery School female instructors. These paddling trips offer women an opportunity to share ideas, techniques, and experiences with each other. Participants will develop valuable wilderness skills and practice techniques for carrying boat and gear.

A **Moose River Canoe Trip** and **The West Branch of the Penobscot** are two popular canoeing adventures exclusively for women.

These L.L. Bean programs are given annually at different times and some are repeated. They may vary from year to year, so it is best to write or call for the latest update or check the Web site. You can call toll free **1-888-LLBEAN (1-888-552-3261)** or check the Web site: **www.llbean.com**. From there, you will be guided to the Outdoor Discovery School to check courses and schedules, and also access other information about canoes, paddles, clothing, and equipment as you wish.

AMERICAN CANOE ASSOCIATION CANOE PROGRAMS

Founded in 1880, the American Canoe Association (ACA) is the oldest and largest nonprofit agency in the country representing the interests of paddlers. Today it supports conservation and river access efforts, education programs, water safety instruction, athletic competition, and much more. Long recognized for its high standards and instruction, the ACA offers a wide range of courses and classes for beginners, intermediate level and up, to developmental workshops for aspiring instructors and trip leaders.

ACA-certified instructors teach students to paddle all kinds of water, from the quiet inlets of millponds to the wild froth of whitewater rivers. They teach students of all ages, from the youngest Girl Scout or summer camper to the oldest retiree. They also teach disabled paddlers and people with all levels of ability, from the absolute novice to the expert who you might see someday racing across the finish line in future Olympic Games.

ACA basic courses are open to all people who are comfortable around the water, except where additional prerequisites are noted. The hours allow coverage of all course material and instructors may teach shorter or longer courses as appropriate to the students in the class and water and weather conditions at the time it is given.

Courses include **Introduction to Paddling,** usually 5 to 8 hours, and **Introduction to River Paddling,** also 5 to 8 hours. There are also 16-hour **Flatwater, Moving Water, and Whitewater** courses.

Freestyle Canoeing is a two-day course that includes most of the flatwater material. **River Safety and Rescue Techniques** is a course for participants who have moderate to strong swimming ability. ACA Instructor Certification workshops are scheduled periodically for those with advanced canoeing skills who seek to upgrade their abilities and become instructors themselves.

In the **Instructor Development Workshop for Canoeing,** candidates will be trained in rescue and group management skills, teaching techniques, strokes, and maneuvers in flatwater canoeing. Instructor Trainers provide feedback through video presentations and on-water exercises to help you prepare for the ACA Instructor Certification Examination. A minimum of one year of paddling and teaching experience is a prerequisite.

The American Canoe Association Instructor Certification Examination evaluates candidates for their readiness to be certified instructors. Participants will teach both on and off the water, give presentations on various topics and manage and lead groups on the water. Those who successfully meet ACA criteria will receive Instructor Certification.

There are more than 3,000 certified ACA instructors living in all parts of the country. Courses are given throughout the year in many areas. You can obtain information about classes, courses, and other sponsored programs directly from the **American Canoe Association at 7432 Alban Station Blvd. Suite 232, Springfield, VA, 22150.** Telephone is **703-451-0141** and FAX is **703-451-2245.** Email **acadirect@aol.com.**

To access some of the best canoeing information and classes, the ACA's Internet site is **www.aca-paddler.org.** That site offers links to many other canoeing topics, clubs, outfitters, and outdoor-related organizations, product manufacturers, and associations. Through the ACA Web site, you also can locate hundreds of affiliated local, state, and regional canoeing clubs and outfitters. As part of member activities, many clubs give periodic courses and sponsor events.

Outfitters may also offer refresher courses for individuals and families that are planning extended excursions. You can contact clubs and outfitters at the addresses, phone numbers and other communications systems provided via the ACA Web site communications links.

Every year, the ACA sponsors and sanctions a wide diversity of exciting, competitive events. *Paddler* magazine and the ACA Newsletter provide details about upcoming events. You also can find news and events easily via the ACA site.

COURSES FOR PADDLERS WITH DISABILITIES

Wilderness Inquiry is a recognized national leader in Universal Design and Program Training. They conduct several types of classes for adventurers with disabilities. One in particular, **Families Integrating Together,** bears special mention. This is a program focused on families who have a member with a disability. The training is aimed at providing families the skills and confidence to perform outdoor recreation, including canoeing, as an integrated unit to include the person with the disability. This inclusion does not minimize the difficulty or the adventure of the experience. It also encourages the family not to segregate their members during outdoor recreation opportunities.

Wilderness Inquiry has been expanding its courses to train workers in local, county, and state parks, YMCA camps and similar organizations and other recreation agencies. Details are available from WI at **1313 Fifth St. SE, Box 84, Minneapolis, MN 55414.** Their Web site is **www.wildernessinquiry.org** and you can find your way to many programs there.

Wilderness Inquiry features canoe adventures for people with disabilities around the United States, including this trip on the Mississippi River. (Courtesy Wilderness Inquiry)

You can gather information to help plan your trip from many sources including outfitters, chambers of commerce, and canoeing associations.

Sources and Information

There are many sources for information about places to go, courses to take, and outfitters that provide exceptional opportunities to canoe in the United States and abroad. Here are some of the best sources.

The *American Canoe Association* is the foremost canoeing organization. Their Web site offers an abundance of information, plus useful links to many other sources. One of the most useful is Water and Weather, a link that connects you to many timely sources. The U.S. Geological Survey (USGS) Streamflow Conditions site provides current water levels across the United States. One of the most helpful sources is a National Water Conditions page. You can use the USGS Water Resources with streamflow data to help plan your trips and be prepared for the water conditions you'll find in various waterways. Other sites update you on water levels and conditions, using data from the Army Corps of Engineers in various states. Tide and lake levels are available from the National Oceanographic and Atmospheric (NOAA). The definitive government weather resource, the National Weather Service, also is accessible, all by links on the ACA Web site.

The **American Canoe Association** is at **7432 Alban Station Blvd. Suite B-232, Springfield, VA 22150. Telephone 703-451-0141, FAX 703-451-2245** and email at **acadirect@aol.com** and Web site **www.aca-paddler.org.**

Annual individual membership is $25, a Sustaining membership is $35, and Family memberships ($40) are available. At the ACA Web site you can access updated lists of competitive canoeing and kayaking events, get-togethers, and news about canoeing, plus tap a list of hundreds of canoeing clubs, conveniently listed by states, with addresses and often phone and email contacts as well. You'll also find lists of product manufacturers, canoeing outfitters, and other topics.

The ACA Paddlesport Industry link lets you look up useful information about canoes, paddles, racks, apparel, and other equipment and supplies for canoeing. In addition, you can connect to federal agencies, including the USDA Forest Service, the National Park Service, the Bureau of Land Management (BLM), and others.

The Outfitters Page is especially useful. From it you can access the most experienced and knowledgeable canoe outfitters in every state. Other useful links on the ACA home page connect you to Great Outdoor Recreation pages, Wilderness Furnishings, and The Wilderness Society and Sierra Club home pages, plus some of the best National Parks Web sites.

The **Professional Paddlesports Association** is another key group. This nationwide, non-profit association is composed of more than 450 of the most knowledgeable professional outfitters in the United States and beyond. PPA is affiliated with the ACA, the American Recreation Coalition, and other associations that relate to the watersports industry. Most members are located in rural areas or small communities. They know their areas, the best waterways, the water conditions, and the flora and fauna that abound there.

The **Professional Paddle Sports Association** at **P.O. Box 248, Butler, Kentucky,** can be phoned at **606-472-2205** or contacted via email at **paddlespt@unidial.com.** The PPA Web site, **www.propaddler.com**, provides names and contacts of outfitters in almost every state.

Chambers of Commerce are anxious to provide you with details about waterway recreation and vacations in their respective areas. You can write or email many in the area you plan to visit. Always allow sufficient time for them to send you brochures, maps, and other information by snail mail.

The **American Automobile Association** also has a wide range of services and information on recreational areas. Their various state and regional magazines also provide helpful articles with email contacts to ask for additional information. AAA offices in your area can help you plan trips and obtain maps, brochures, and other useful information, wherever you want to go.

State Tourism Information

State Tourism Boards and Offices gladly provide a wealth of free information about their states. Here's the list, with toll-free numbers. You also can find information fast on the Internet, by looking up state tourist information.

Alabama Bureau of Tourism and Travel	800-ALABAMA
Alaska Division of Tourism	907-465-2010
Arizona Office of Tourism	602-230-7733
Arkansas Department of Parks and Tourism	800-NATURAL
California Division of Tourism	800-862-2543
Connecticut Tourism Office	800-282-6863
Delaware Tourism Office	800-441-8846
Florida Division of Tourism	904-263-3510
Georgia Department of Tourism	800-VISIT-GA
Hawaii Visitors Bureau	808-923-1811
Idaho Department of Commerce	800-635-7820
Illinois Bureau of Tourism	800-822-0292
Indiana Division of Tourism	800-759-9191
Iowa Division of Tourism	800-345-4692
Kansas Travel and Tourism Development	800-2-KANSAS

Kentucky Department of Travel Development	800-225-TRIP
Louisiana Office of Tourism	800-633-6970
Maine Publicity Bureau	800-553-9595
Maryland Office of Tourism	800-719-5900
Massachusetts Office of Tourism	617-727-3201
Michigan Travel Bureau	800-5432-YES
Minnesota Office of Tourism	800-657-3700
Mississippi Tourism Division	800-WARMEST
Missouri Division of Tourism	800-877-1234
Travel Montana	800-VISIT-MT
Nebraska Division of Travel and Tourism	800-228-4307
Nevada Commission on Tourism	800-NEVADA-8
New Hampshire Office of Tourism	800-FUN-IN-NH
New Jersey Division of Travel and Tourism	800-JERSEY-7
New Mexico Department of Tourism	800-545-2040
New York State Division of Tourism	800-CALL-NYS
North Carolina Travel and Tourism Division	800-VISIT-NC
North Dakota Tourism	800-435-5663
Ohio Division of Travel and Tourism	800-BUCKEYE
Oklahoma Tourism and Recreation Department	800-652-6552
Oregon Tourism Division	800-547-7842
Pennsylvania Office of Travel Marketing	800-VISIT-PA
Rhode Island Tourism Division	800-556-2484
South Carolina Division of Tourism	800-734-0122
South Dakota Tourism	800-SDAKOTA
Tennessee Tourist Development	615-741-2158
Texas Tourism Division	800-452-9292
Utah Travel Council	800-200-1160
Vermont Travel Division	800-VERMONT
Virginia Division of Tourism	800-932-5827
Washington Tourism Development	800-544-1800
West Virginia Division of Tourism	800-CALL-WVA
Wisconsin Division of Tourism	800-432-TRIP
Wyoming Division of Tourism	800-CALL-WYO

CANADIAN TOURIST OFFICES

Alberta Economic Development/Tourism	800-661-8888
Tourism British Columbia	800-663-6000
Travel Manitoba	800-665-0040
New Brunswick Tourism	800-561-0123
Newfoundland and Labrador	800-563-6353
Nova Scotia Department of Tourism	800-565-0000
Ontario Travel	800-ONTARIO
Prince Edward Island	800-463-4PEI
Tourisme Quebec	800-363-7777
Tourism Saskatchewan	877-237-2273

WEBSITE REFERENCES AND RESOURCES

American Canoe Association	**www.aca-paddler.org**
Professional Paddlesports Association	**www.propaddle.com**
L.L. Bean	**www.llbean.com**
American Automobile Association	**www.aaa.com**
National Wildlife Federation	**www.nationalwildlife.org**
National Park Service	**www.nps.gov**
USDA Forest Service	**www.fs.fed.us**
Bureau of Land Management	**www.blm.gov**
National Audubon Society	**www.audubon.org**
Old Town Canoe	**www.otccanoe.com**
Sierra Club	**www.sierraclub.org**
Wilderness Inquiry	**www.wildernessinquiry.org**
Native Trails—Canoeing	**www.nativetrails.org**
Rutabaga Paddler's	**www.paddlers.com**

The L.L. Bean Web site now provides one of the best sources for finding places to canoe all across America. Just connect to L.L. Bean at **www.llbean.com** and click into Parks. In 1999, that provided a link to a page that listed 782 state parks, 163 national parks, 151 national forests, 297 national wildlife refuges, and 98 Bureau of Land Management lands.

You can search for a particular park by name, location, or even activity. If you click on activity, you can select Canoeing. That provided more than 880 parks and lands nationwide. From that point you can access and print out details on individual parks. For example, at the Web site for the Delaware Water Gap National Recreation Area, which divides New Jersey and Pennsylvania, you'll find much useful information. Details about hiking, fishing, canoeing, boating, swimming, and other activities on 60 trails, including a 25-mile stretch of the Appalachian Mountain Trail. Historic sites, public and private campground information is provided.

For the Alligator River National Wildlife Refuge in Manteo, North Carolina, you'll find details about 150,000 acres of wetland habitats and information about paddling the creeks and canals of the Alligator River trail system.

Paddle where you wish among these Web sites. There's a world of adventure awaiting you.

A little planning goes a long way toward a fun-filled vacation.

Glossary

Aft   Refers to the stern or rear of the canoe.

Air lock   A suction that occurs in the hull of a canoe when it is overturned in the water, which makes it difficult to right.

Amidship   The center of a boat.

Back ferry   Back paddling with your canoe at angle to the current during down-stream run in order to cross a stream or river.

Backlash   Standing waves at the foot of a powerful chute or sluice that are created when fast-flowing water strikes relatively still or calm water.

Banana boat   A term describing a decked canoe or kayak-type craft with an upswept keel line, designed for high maneuverability.

Beam   The width of the craft at its widest point.

Blade   The flat section of a canoe paddle.

Boil   Water swelling upward, usually upon striking an underwater object such as a rock or log.

Bow   The front end of a canoe or other watercraft.

Brace stroke   A stroke during which a canoeist leans far out of the canoe to effect a quick turn. It is primarily a whitewater stroke.

Bridle   A line run loosely under the forward end of a canoe, from gunwale to gunwale, to which a towing line is attached.

Broach   To turn broadside to oncoming waves or current.

Canoe pole   A wooden or aluminum pole used to propel a canoe in shallow water.

Carry   Term for a portage.

Channel   A navigable route among obstructions in a stream.

Chine   The curving section of a canoe's sides where they bend or merge at the bottom.

Chute   An accelerated section of a stream, often compressed between two or more obstructions and dropping faster than adjacent current.

Classification   A rating system applied to a stream or section of current describing its navigability. Classes are described on pages 125–126.

Cutwater   The front end of the canoe that cuts through the water.

Dead man   A log, anchored at one end, afloat at the other, usually found on streams where log drives have occurred.

Deck   A triangular section fitted between the gunwales at the bow and stern of paddling canoes. Canoes used for whitewater sometimes have a **running deck,** a full covering to prevent water coming over the sides, with a cockpit area for the canoeist.

Decked canoe   One with a full covering, end to end.

Draft   Depth of water required to float a canoe or boat, or the vertical distance between the waterline and the keel.

Drip rings   Leather or metal rings on the shaft of a double paddle to prevent water from running down the shaft. Most often used on kayak paddles, but some solo canoeists like to use kayak paddles.

Drop   A sudden pitch or usually sharp dip in a section of a rapids.

Dry pack   A waterproof bag for carrying clothing. Mostly used by whitewater canoeists.

Duffek stroke   Similar to a brace stroke.

Eddy   A section of a current, downstream of a major obstruction, where water flows in a circular course.

Eddy line   A fine line between downstream current and a circulating or upstream current within an eddy.

Fast water   Generally considered to mean rapids, but can also be applied to swiftly flowing water without obstructions.

Feather   To bring a paddle forward with one edge leading, thus reducing resistance to water or air.

Ferry   To cross a river by holding a canoe at an angle to the current and paddling.

Flare   The section of a canoe paddle where the shaft widens to become the blade.

Flotation   Styrofoam, float bags, inner tubes or similar devices or substances placed in canoes to provide buoyancy.

Float plan   A written itinerary of put-in point, waterway paddling and camping sites, take-out point, and the date to complete trip and return home. Should be left with a family member or friend and a warden at waterway site in case of emergency.

Foldboat   A collapsible kayak-like watercraft.

Following sea   Waves that overtake a craft from astern, usually wind driven.

Forward ferry   A foward paddle stroke with the canoe at an angle to current, used to cross a stream.

Freeboard   The height of a canoe side above waterline, measured at the middle of the canoe.

Gauging station   A streamside device for measuring flow of water in a river.

Gilpoke   An old lumberman's term for a log protruding into a stream.

Gradient   The average rate of drop in a river, generally expressed in feet per mile.

Grip   The top of a canoe paddle shaft, shaped roughly to fit the hand. There are several different types and shapes of grips.

Gunwale(s)   The strips along the top of a canoe's sides, extending from bow to stern.

Haystack   Another term for backlash, standing waves at the foot of a powerful chute where fast water strikes calmer water.

Hog   A canoe that is overly bow-heavy. It also applies to a craft whose keel line is higher amidship than at either end.

Hull   The main body of a canoe.

Inwale   The inside gunwale.

Kayak   A decked watercraft with one or more cockpits for occupants, usually with a V or semi-V bottom and low ends.

Keel   The bottom center line of a canoe, running from bow to stern, designed to prevent slide-slipping. It may be molded into a canoe hull, or attached on some.

Ledge   A projecting stratum of rock, which confines or partially dams a stream's flow.

Lee   A section of waterway that is sheltered from wind.

Lining   Guiding a canoe downstream through rough water or shallow water by means of a rope or line.

Outwale   The outside gunwale.

Painter   A length of rope attached to either or both ends of a boat.

Pick pole   Another term for a canoe pole.

Pillow   A bulge on the surface of a river created by an underwater obstruction, usually a rock or sunken log.

Pitch   A steep section of water, usually of rapids as the river drops to a lower level.

Poling   Propelling a canoe with a pole.

Port   The left side of a watercraft facing forward.

Portage   To carry the canoe on shore around a stream obstruction or between two waterways. The portage, or **carry**, may also refer to the route followed over land when carrying the canoe.

Power face   The side of a paddle blade that pushes against the water during a stroke.

Rapids   Swiftly flowering water, tumbling with some degree of force among obstructions and creating turbulence.

Riffles   Swift, shallow water running over a gravel or sand bottom and creating small waves. A term for gentle rapids.

Rips   Moderate rapids.

River rating   Another term for **classification**, a system of ranking difficulty of a river to canoe.

Rock garden   Navigable rock-strewn rapids.

Rocker   The upward sweep of the keel line toward both ends of a canoe, characteristic of river craft.

Rollers   Another term for **backlash.**

Scouting   Appraising rapids before running them in your canoe.

Setting pole   Another term for **canoe pole.**

Shaft   The handle of a canoe paddle, between the grip and the blade.

Slack water   Stream flow without rapids or riffles.

Slalom   A zigzag course, usually set up in rapids for competition, much like slalom courses for downhill skiing.

Snubbing   Stopping or slowing the canoe's momentum with a canoe pole while running downstream.

Souse hole   A frothy, high-foamed; eddy, or a depressed surface of water downstream of a large obstruction; generally found in a fast-flowing stream.

Spray cover   A temporary fabric deck used on open canoes during whitewater running to keep the craft from taking on water.

Spray skirt   A fabric sleeve which encloses a paddler's waist and is attached to the spray cover.

Starboard   The right-hand side of the watercraft facing forward.

Stem   The entire bow, the curved section of frame which forms the **cutwater**.

Throat   The flaring of the paddle shaft where it starts to form the blade.

Thwart   The cross braces running from gunwale to gunwale that provide reinforcement for the sides of the canoe.

Tip   The bottom end of a canoe paddle blade.

Tracking   Towing a canoe upstream by hand with line; and also refers to paddling in a straight line.

Trim   The manner in which a canoe rides on the water.

Trip leader   The canoeist in charge of a trip.

Trough   The depression between waves.

Tumblehome   The inboard curvature of a canoe's sides, from the keel or bottom to the gunwale.

Waterline   The level water reaches on the canoe's sides when it is carrying a normal load.

Wet suit   A protective, close-fitting suit that serves to insulate the paddler against cold water in case of upset or overturning.

White eddy   A pool at the foot of a drop over which water flows that creates a marked backflow on the surface, usually highly aerated and somewhat less buoyant than other water surfaces.

White water   Rapids.

Windward   The direction from which the wind is coming.

Yoke   A device attached permanently or temporarily amidship; usually padded to protect the paddlers' shoulders when portaging a canoe.

Avoid unmanageable suprises on the water. Always know the classifications of the river you wish to paddle.

River Type Classifications

Whenever and wherever you go to canoe, it pays to ask knowledgeable local people about the conditions and classification of the river, in the season you plan to canoe. The best sources are local canoeing outfitters, guides, and sporting goods stores. Other reliable sources are local Fire and Rescue organizations, often staffed by knowledgeable and outdoor-minded men and women who know their local rivers at different times of the year.

The International River Classification System has been established to provide positive identification that measures the various difficulties you may find on white water. It is an established guide for safety. Add to this information a basic paddling premise: Remember that your experience, skill level, judgement, and precautions are the most vital factors as you approach each type of water.

- **Class I:** *Very easy.* Waves are small and regular. Passages clear. There may be sandbanks or artificial difficulties like docks and bridge piers or pilings and some riffles.

- **Class II:** *Easy.* There may be rapids of medium difficulty with sufficient passages clear and wide and possibly low ledges to navigate around.

- **Class III:** *Medium difficulty.* Waves may be numerous and high. The river is lined with irregular rocks, eddies, and rapids with narrow but mostly clear areas for passage. For this type of water you'll need some expertise in maneuvering your canoe. Although inspection of the waterway usually isn't needed, it is advisable in spring runoff periods and after heavy storms.

- **Class IV:** *Difficult.* You'll find long rapids, powerful waves, irregular and sometimes dangerous rocks and often boiling eddies. Passages are more difficult to inspect but inspect you should. For this class, you will need precise, powerful, and determined maneuvering skills.

- **Class V:** *Dangerous.* Usually considered uncanoeable except by seasoned, daring experts with covered or especially equipped canoes. Unless you are an expert and have paid-up insurance, avoid Class IV and any more dangerous waters. Canoeing should be fun, not life-threatening.

Rapids can be a fun challenge to paddle—or to relax by and observe.

Acknowledgments

This book began in a canoe years ago with the idea of helping others enjoy worthwhile outdoor adventures and wilderness discoveries in their canoes as I had been launched as a youngster. The author gratefully acknowledges the advice, wit, and wisdom of many canoeists who helped me paddle my first canoe, enjoy America's magnificent waterways and write this book to share my knowledge and theirs with others.

Special thanks to the talented canoeing instructors at the L.L. Bean Outdoor Discovery School: Jackie Peppe, Karen Knight, Kathy Kurz, Bob Myron, Jamey Galloway, and Ed Maillett at the L.L. Bean store in Freeport. They were a constant inspiration and responded graciously whenever I asked for some help and advice.

Many thanks also to Jim Kaiser of Old Town Canoes, Sandy Martin of Lincoln Canoes, Corey Schlosser-Hall of Wilderness Inquiry, Mike Krepner of Native Trails, the enthusiastic canoeists at the American Canoe Association and Paddlesports organization, plus many others who offered advice and tuned me into super good information on their Web sites and through email connections around the entire country. It is a pleasure to salute you and list your companies, organizations, and Web sites in the special Sources and Information section at the end of this book, so others can benefit from your thoughtfulness, knowledge, and resourcefulness as they embark on their own canoeing adventures.

Allan A. Swenson

About the Author

Allan A. Swenson is the author of 50 published books about nature, outdoor adventures, the environment, and gardening. He has also written many children's books on those topics.

Some of his outdoor books for families and children include *World Beneath Your Feet, World Above Your Head, World Within a Tidal Pool, Secrets of a Seashore, America's Wolves Today, Hurrah for Christopher, Thar She Blows, Vacation Fun Guide, Babes in the Woods, Seagull's Day, Wood Heat,* and *Guide To Animals.*

An avid outdoorsman and naturalist, he attended the National Boy Scouts of America training school and became a waterfront and canoeing instructor while in college. He extended his outdoor knowledge as an Army Airborne Officer with Special Forces survival skills training, which he incorporates in his outdoor writing.

He has canoed lakes and rivers around the United States and continues his outdoor activities and writing for newspapers, national magazines, and his books. Also a multimedia personality, Swenson has appeared on the CBS, NBC, and CBN networks on topics related to his books.

He currently is writing a Nature Watchers Page with Internet distribution as The Old Woodsman from his Viking Ridge Farm in Maine. Other upcoming books include *Wilderness Skills and Survival Guide* and *Leif Landed First,* the story of the original discovery of the New World by Leif Ericson in 1000 A.D., 400 years before Columbus was born.

The world of wilderness adventure awaits you.

Index

Above waterline canoe design, 20–21
Adventures, canoeing, 5–14. *See also*
       Camping; Excursions; Natural
       discoveries
Allagash Waterway, 7
  five day excursion, 108
  seven day excursion, 109
American Automobile Association, 114
American Canoe Association (ACA), 5,
       109
  contact information, 113–114
  course offerings and certification
       programs, 110–111
Animal(s)
  bald eagles, 77, 79
  bank swallows, 79
  bass, 86
  beavers, 80
  bluegills, 86
  catfish, 86
  deer, 82
  fishing for supper, 86–87
  kingfishers, 79
  moose, 81
  perch, 86
  peregrine falcon, 79
  raccoons, 79
  river otters, 80
  rock bass, 86
  sunfish, 86
  tracks of, 82
    casting, 82–83
    identifying, 84–85
  wood ducks, 79

Bald eagles, 77, 79
Bank swallows, 79
Bass, 86
Bear Creek canoes, 23
Beavers, 80
Bluegills, 86
Boarding canoe, 33
Boundary Waters, 13

Campfire considerations, 70–71
Camping, 59
  campfire considerations, 70–71
  checklists for, 73–75
  cooking fuels, 68–69
  etiquette for, 93
  leave- no-trace, principles and
      programs, 90–93
  lighting considerations, 71–72
  meal preparation, 65–66

checklist for, 74–75
    food menu and ideas, 66–68
    keeping foods cool, 65
minimal use of campsites, 92
setting up camp, 65–66
site selection, 60
stove types and considerations, 68
tents, tarps, sleeping bags
    care and maintenance, 63–64
    professional recommendations, 62
    selection of, 61–63
wild animal considerations, 72–73
Canadian tourist offices, 117
Canoe(s)
aluminum, 17
American tradition of, 1–3
categories of, 15–16
construction of, *See* Canoe materials
derivation of word, 1
design of, *See* Canoe design
fiberglass, 16
handling, *See* Canoeing techniques;
    Stroke techniques
names of parts of, 18
paddling, *See* Stroke techniques
parts of, 18
performance variables of, 19
polyethylene-ABS, 17
portaging, 2
purchasing points, 21–25
recommended models of,
    professionally, 22–23
recreational, 15
rescue with, 45
river-running, 15
sporting, 16
terminology of, 18
touring, 16
tripping, 15
use of, *See* Canoeing techniques
wood-canvas, 16
wood strip, 16
Canoe design, 17–19
    above waterline, 20–21
    cross-sectional shape, 19–20

hull, 20
keel, 19
part names in, 18
Canoe materials
aluminum, 17
fiberglass, 16
polyethylene-ABS, 17
wood-canvas, 16
wood strip, 16
Canoeing
adventures in, 5–14, *See also*
        Camping; Excursions; Natural
        discoveries
    recommended by Outdoor
        Discovery School, 11
clothing for, *See* Clothing
equipment for, *See* Canoe(s); Paddles;
    Personal flotation devices
excursions for, *See* Excursions
gear and accessories for, *See* Gear, and
    accessories
lessons in, *See* Lessons
safety precautions in, *See* Safety
solo, *See* Excursions; Stroke
    techniques
stroke techniques in, basic, 34–42,
        See also Stroke techniques
tandem, *See* Excursions; Stroke
    techniques
terminology of, 18
Canoeing techniques, 31
    basic canoeing strokes, 34–42, *See
        also* Stroke techniques, basic
    boarding canoe, 33
    capsizing and recovery, 43–45
    loading/unloading from car roof, 31
    practicing, 42
    single-person carry, 32
Canyonlands' Green River, 9
Capsizing, and recovery techniques,
        43–45
Carry, single-person, 32
Catfish, 86
Checklist(s)
    for camping, 73–75

for clothing, 51–52

for day trips, gear and accessories, 53–54

for meal preparation, in camping, 74–75

for overnight, gear and accessories, 54–55

safety supply, 101

Children's canoeing lessons, 106

Clothing, 47–48

checklist for, 51–52

considerations in choosing

protection of extremities, 50–51

warmth, 48–49

weather, 48

wicking, 49–50

fabric information, 57

gear and accessories, 52–55

professional recommendations for, 55–56

Cold water, 97

Cooking. *See* Camping; Meal preparation; Stove types

Cooking fuels, 68–69

Coosa Trail, 13

Cross-sectional shape, 19–20

Crossbow draw stroke, 40

CrossLink3, 16–17

Day trips, 108. *See also* Excursions

gear and accessories for, 53–54

leave- no-trace, principles and programs, 90–93

lessons, 106

Deer, 82

Dehydration, 96

Draw stroke, 39

Draw to bow, 39

Draw to stern, 40

Drinking water, 96

Dugouts, 1

Eastern Ohio Trail, 13

Ecosytems, avoiding damage to, 90–91, 92

Environmental stewardship, 89

Boy Scouts of America program in, 93

leave-no-trace principles, 90–93

Excursions

American Canoeing Association, 109–111

leave- no-trace, principles and programs, 90–93

Outdoor Discovery School, 103

Allagash Trip, five day, 108

Allagash Trip, seven day, 109

day tripping, 108

Moose River canoe trip, 108

professional recommendations from, 11

West Branch of Penobscot, 108

women's only, 109

Explorer line models, 23

Fabric information, clothing, 57

Families Integrating Together, 111

First aid lessons, wilderness, 107

Fish

bass, 86

bluegills, 86

catfish, 86

perch, 86

rock bass, 86

sunfish, 86

Fishing, for supper, 86–87

Flare design, 20–21

Foldboat, 1

Forward one-quarter sweep, 38

Forward stroke, 35–36

Forward sweep, 38

Freestyle solo canoeing, lessons, 104

Freestyle tandem canoeing, lessons, 104

Gear, and accessories, 52

checklist for day trips, 53–54

checklist for overnight, and longer, 54–55

Glossary, 119–123

Grips, paddle, 27–28

Hull design, 20
Hull shape, canoe, 21

Information sources, 113, 118
    American Automobile Association,
        114
    American Canoe Association, 113
    Canadian Tourist Offices, 117
    Professional Paddlesports
        Association, 114
    State Tourism Information, 115–116
    Web sites, 117

J-stroke, 36–37
Juniper Springs, 6

Keel design, 19
Kevlar canoes, 16–17
Kingfishers, 79

Labyrinth Canyon, 9
Lake George, 6
Land owners, permission from, 93
Leave- no-trace, principles and
        programs, 90–93
Length, canoe, 21
Lessons
    American Canoe Association,
        109–110
    Outdoor Discovery School, 103
        children's canoeing, 106
        day trips, 106
        freestyle solo canoeing, 104
        freestyle tandem canoeing, 104
        map and compass, level I, 106
        map and compass, level II, 106
        moving water workshop for
            tandem canoeing, 105
        parent and child overnight, 106
        quick-starting canoe, 104
        solo paddling, 103
        tandem canoeing, 104
        wilderness first aid, 107
    for paddlers with disabilities, 111
    Wilderness Inquiry, 111

Lighting, for camping, 71–72
Lincoln canoes, 23
LL Bean Web site, 117
Loading/unloading, from car roof, 31
Lost persons, 98–100

Mad River canoes, models of, 23
Map and compass
    level I lessons, 106
    level II lessons, 106
Meal preparation, in camping, 65–66
    checklist for, 74–75
    food menu and ideas, 66–68
    keeping foods cool, 65
Mineral Bottoms, 9
Missouri Breaks, 13
Missouri River, 7
Moose, 81
Moose River, 6
Moose River canoe trip, 108
Moving water workshop, for tandem
        canoeing, 105

Namekagon River, 7
Native Trails Inc., 13
Natural discoveries, 77
    animal tracks, 82
        casting, 82–83
        identifying, 84–85
    bald eagles, 77, 79
    bank swallows, 79
    bass, 86
    beavers, 80
    bluegills, 86
    catfish, 86
    deer, 82
    fishing for supper, 86–87
    kingfishers, 79
    moose, 81
    perch, 86
    peregrine falcon, 79
    raccoons, 79
    river otters, 80
    rock bass, 86
    sunfish, 86

wood ducks, 79
Northern Forest Canoe Trail, 9–10, 13

Ocala National Forest, 6
Ocklawaha River, 6
Old Town canoes, models of, 22
Osprey model, 22
Outdoor Discovery School, 11
    excursions
        Allagash Trip, five day, 108
        Allagash Trip, seven day, 109
        day tripping, 108
        Moose River canoe trip, 108
        West Branch of Penobscot, 108
        women's only, 109
        lessons
        children's canoeing, 106
        day trips, 106
        freestyle solo paddling, 104
        freestyle tandem paddling, 104
        map and compass, level I, 106
        map and compass, level II, 106
        moving water workshop for
          tandem paddling, 105
        paddling solo, 103
        parent and child overnight, 106
        quick-starting canoe, 104
        tandem canoeing, 104
        wilderness first aid, 107
Overnight trips, gear and accessories for,
    54–55

Pack it in, pack it out, 91
Paddles
    blade choice and types, 26–27
    grip types, 27–28
    materials in, 26
    parts of, 24
    shaft sizing, 25
    types of, 24
Paddling. *See* Stroke techniques
Parent and child overnight camping
    lessons, 106
Penobscot model, 22
Perch, 86

Peregrine falcon, 79
Performance variables, 19
Personal flotation devices (PFDs), 28.
    See also Safety
    care of, 29
    requirements regarding, 28
    types of, 29
PFDs. *See* Personal flotation devices
Potomac Heritage Trail, 13
Practicing strokes/techniques, 42
Preparation, and planning, 90
Professional Paddle Sports Association,
    114
Pry stroke, 41
Purchasing points, canoe, 21–25

Quick-starting canoe lessons, 104

Raccoons, 79
Reentering canoe, from water, 43–44
Rescue, performing canoe, 45
Reverse one-quarter sweep, 38
River classifications, 125–126
River otters, 80
Rock bass, 86

Safety, considerations for canoeing,
    95–96
    cold water, 97
    dehydration, 96
    drinking water, 96
    lost persons, 98–100
    supply checklist, 101
    weather, 97
        lightning, 98
        signs and signals, 97–98
Setting up camp, 65–66
Side stroke, 41
Sideslip, 42
Silver Springs, 6
Single-person carry, 32
Site selection, for camping, 60
Sleeping bags. *See* Tents, tarps, sleeping
    bags
Solo canoeing lessons, 103

Sources, information, 113, 118
   American Automobile Association,
      114
   American Canoe Association, 113
   Canadian Tourist Offices, 117
   Professional Paddlesports
      Association, 114
   State Tourism Information, 115–116
   Web sites, 117
St. Croix River (Wisconsin and Maine),
   7
State tourism information, 115–116
Stillwater model, 22
Stove types, camping, 68
Stroke techniques, basic, 34–35
   crossbow draw stroke, 40
   draw stroke, 39
   draw to bow, 39
   draw to stern, 40
   forward one-quarter sweep, 38
   forward stroke, 35–36
   forward sweep, 38
   J-stroke, 36–37
   practicing, 42
   pry stroke, 41
   reverse one-quarter sweep, 38
   side stroke, 41
   terminology of, 34–35
Sunfish, 86
Supply checklist, 101

Tandem canoeing lessons, 104
Ten Thousand Islands, 6

Tents, tarps, sleeping bags
   care and maintenance, 63–64
   professional recommendations, 62
   selection of, 61–63
Tourism information
   Canadian, 117
   state, 115–116
   Web sites, 117
Tumblehome design, 20–21

U.S. Geological Survey, 113

Weather, 97
   lightning, 98
   signs and signals, 97–98
Web sites, 117
West Branch of Penobscot excursion,
   108
Widow makers, 60
Width, canoe, 21
Wild animals, and camping, 72–73,
   92–93. *See also* Safety
Wilderness adventures, 5–14. *See also*
      Camping; Excursions; Natural
      discoveries
Wilderness first aid lessons, 107
Wilderness Inquiry, 111
Women's only excursions, 109
Wood ducks, 79

Yellowstone National Park, 9